A SOCIAL PSYCHOLOGY OF EDUCATION

ALAN EDWARD GUSKIN
UNIVERSITY OF MICHIGAN

SAMUEL LOUIS GUSKIN
INDIANA UNIVERSITY

ADDISON-WESLEY PUBLISHING COMPANY

Reading, Massachusetts

Menlo Park, California • London • Don Mills, Ontario

This book is in the

ADDISON-WESLEY SERIES IN EDUCATION
Social, Behavioral, and Philosophical Foundations

Consulting Editor
Byron G. Massialas

We dedicate this book to:
our parents, David and Frances Guskin,
our wives, Judith and Phyllis,
and our children, Sharon, Karen, and Jane.

FOREWORD

This series is designed primarily for those who will assume leadership roles in the schools of today—the teachers. In a rapidly changing world, schools are required to develop new educational roles and perspectives; more than ever before they pay attention, directly or indirectly, to the social, political, and economic conditions of the larger society. In this new era, education is considered to be an investment in national development, and equalitarian principles increasingly provide the basis for educational policies. Such factors as the socio-economic status of children, their ethnicity, regional differences, occupational aspirations, and their beliefs and values have been gaining in importance. These and similar factors determine to a large extent the educational environment needed to generate in children a motivation to learn, to think critically, and to develop defensible ideas about themselves and society.

Consciously or unconsciously, teachers impart norms of the individual's role in society. Regardless of their subject of instruction, teachers have, for example, the potential for performing a political socialization function—they are in a position to convey to children knowledge about and attitudes toward the political system. Children begin, at a very young age, to internalize the political norms which characterize the system; e.g., participation, social trust, political efficacy, etc.

It is our firm belief that an effective teacher should become thoroughly familiar both with the substantive content of certain of these topics and issues and with the role of the school in dealing effectively with emerging social problems. In turn, the teacher's role is not only to introduce these topics and issues in the context of civilization's past wisdom, but to motivate the student to seek new viewpoints and solutions through his own inquiry skills and creative talents. It is not presumptuous to reaffirm that mankind's future largely depends on the quantity and quality of education of our youth.

Specifically, the books in this series are designed to help the reader understand the following:

1) The functions of education as a social agency and its interrelations with other social agencies.

2) The historical roles of schools and changes in these roles mainly resulting from urbanization and industrialization.

3) The role of education both as an institution and as a process, as it affects personality formation, socialization, cognitive development, and the self-concept of the individual.

4) The impact of education on the social, economic, political, and intellectual development of a nation.

5) The influence of education on human values—their formation, justification, adjudication.

In connection with the above, the series attempts to indicate how knowledge-claims in the field have evolved and what particular skills and procedures of social research have been used. The focus is on selected unifying concepts, e.g., socialization, culture diffusion, elite formation, human values, and economic and political modernization as they relate to education. Each volume singles out an aspect of the relation between education and society and deals with it in depth. Each author, while looking at his topic from the perspective of a scholarly discipline, be it history, political science, sociology, or philosophy, tries to draw from other related fields as well.

We hope that these volumes will offer educators and teachers new insights into our understanding of education and the emerging world culture and will open new doors for additional work and study in the social, behavioral, and philosophical foundations of education.

Byron G. Massialas

PREFACE

Student revolts, teacher strikes, parent demonstrations, financial emergencies, court suits, and major technological changes are becoming expected events in education. Soon the university or school system without a crisis will be viewed as the exception rather than the rule. The pressures on the schools to change and to resist change are tremendous. In some communities the conflict is between the demands of black parents for racial integration and the horror of white parents at this possibility. In other communities, in the large cities, it is the desire of black parents or pupils for local black control over curricula, faculty selection, freedom to dress as they please, and reduction in racial discrimination in extracurricular organizations. Teachers in some places are putting up a strong fight against programmed instruction and other innovations.

While these phenomena can be partially understood at the level of societal structure, e.g., the influence of restricted occupational and residential opportunities on the black community's reactions to schools, and partially at the individual level, e.g., the feeling of powerlessness of the individual pupil as it influences his achievement in school, we feel that it is also extremely important to examine these problems at the interpersonal level, at the point where groups and other individuals bring influence to bear on the individual pupil, teacher, or administrator. In the first six chapters we will focus on the point of interchange between persons and indicate how it affects the individuals involved. We shall try to present certain general ways of viewing behavior change in schools and will try to apply these principles to critical problems in education today. For example, when we examine how a teacher's expectations about a child's performance influence the way the child learns in school, we shall illustrate this with the special case of the lower class black pupil. In the last two chapters we will be concerned with the influence of the social structure of the school upon interpersonal processes and the development of individuals. We will also indicate ways in which the organizational structure of the school can be changed.

One final point. We are not presenting either dogma nor, for that matter, scientifically demonstrated conclusions. We intend this book to be a presentation of ways of conceptualizing educational problems and we have attempted to suggest ways of coping with such problems. We hope that the reader will critically evaluate the applicability of these social psychological approaches to educational problems with which he is personally concerned.

Ann Arbor, Michigan   A.E.G.
Bloomington, Indiana   S.L.G.
March 1970

ACKNOWLEDGMENTS

We would like to thank the many persons who read and commented upon earlier drafts of this manuscript, including our students in a graduate course at Indiana University in Social Psychology in Education and in a freshman course in the Residential College at the University of Michigan. We also owe Matthew Miles a great deal for his detailed critique and encouragement on an earlier draft. Finally, we thank the many secretaries and assistants who contributed during the writing of the book. Although we cannot begin to list the names of all who have helped, we are especially grateful to Margaret McConahy, who gave a great deal of her personal time and was an invaluable aid in the final editing and rewriting of the manuscript.

CONTENTS

CHAPTER ONE

THE ROLE PERSPECTIVE

Though there is no single perspective which can be labeled *the* social psychological viewpoint, there are certain ways of conceptualizing behavior which tend to dominate social psychological thinking and writing. One of these approaches is what is loosely called "role theory." The role perspective attempts to explain behavior by noting how a person's actions derive from his social position and from the obligations and privileges of his position. The social position for which expectations are held may be as general as adult male American or as specific as teacher of sixth grade in P.S. 200. The expectations may be as explicit as a job description or as informal and implicit as the desires that parents hold for their children. What is important is the role-theory assumption that organizational or societal expectations control the actions of individuals in a given position in much the same way as the script controls the performance of actors in a given role. This contrasts with the personality-theory assumption that an individual's behavior can be accounted for by his unique characteristics. This difference in orientation can be clarified by examining the following hypothetical situation.

It is the first day of school in a seventh grade classroom in a large city school. The teacher, who has taught in this school for five years, calls on a boy toward the back of the room to write a word on the blackboard. The student refuses, telling the teacher to "go to hell." The teacher moves rapidly up the aisle between the desks, grabs the boy by the back of the collar, drags and pushes him out of the room, and closes the door behind him. Out in the hall, the teacher pushes the boy against the wall, grabs the front of the boy's collar, lifts him off the ground, whispers what are obviously curses and threats, then lets him down, opens the door again, and pushes the boy in front of him back into the room.

How should we explain what happened? We can seek the answers in the personalities of teacher and pupil or in the demands of their social positions. Is this an impulsive, aggressive, hostile child who is expressing a need to rebel against authority, or is this student conforming to his classmates' expectations that he should not cooperate? Is the teacher an authoritarian individual with strong hostile feelings and intolerance of rule-breaking, or is the teacher doing what he feels must be done to keep his job?

There is not enough information provided about this situation to support either set of interpretations. What sort of evidence would be required to demonstrate the validity of each explanation? Since personality refers to the unique behavior shown by individuals, the appropriateness of a personality interpretation can be demonstrated by showing that several people faced with the same situation handle it differently and that the same person acts consistently when he moves from situation to situation. Thus we would be justified in attributing to the student's personality his refusal to obey instructions and his hostile comment if (1) most other children in the class would have passively obeyed the teacher if called on and (2) this boy had been observed in many other situations to act in a hostile and rebellious manner when asked by any adult to do anything.

In contrast, we would look to role determinants if (1) most other children in the class would also have responded aggressively if called on and (2) this boy had been observed to behave nonaggressively in his relationships with adults outside the classroom. In other words, one can identify a person's behavior as role performance by demonstrating that most people in the same position and situation behave in the same way and that the same person behaves differently when he participates in different positions. Let us apply this principle to the teacher in the above situation: his aggressive response to the boy can be called role behavior if we observe that most of the male teachers in his school respond aggressively to such rebellious behavior in class and that this teacher shows little aggressiveness toward teenagers outside of school. To be certain of this role interpretation, one would want evidence that these teachers feel this behavior is appropriate and expected of them. We could have such evidence if they told us, in confidence, that what the teacher did was what any other teacher in his school would have done, that they needed to maintain discipline, that by doing this the teacher would be able to maintain order in his class for the rest of the term, and that if he had tolerated such student behavior or if he had brought the student's behavior to the attention of the principal instead of coping directly with it, the principal would have seen him as unable to handle his class.

One final point should be made in this comparison between role and personality perspectives. The two types of explanation are not mutually exclusive. In most situations, role demands leave open more than one acceptable pattern of behavior, and the particular choice taken may reflect the personality of the individual "actor," just as on the stage the same script can result in very different performances. In our illustration, the student could have found passive means of being noncooperative, and the teacher could have used more subtle threats to control the pupil.

THE ROLE OF THE TEACHER

Following our definition of role, we can view the "role of the teacher" as any or all of the following: (1) teacher behavior which is a result of what others (society, fellow teachers, the school administration) demand of him; (2) teacher behavior which results from teacher beliefs about what a teacher should do; or (3) the behavior common to most teachers in specified settings such as the classroom.

Shared Inaccuracies in Role Perception

How can one systematically investigate the role of the teacher? One approach is illustrated in a study by Biddle and his associates (1966). They collected information to evaluate whether teachers' behavior matches what teachers believe to be the expectations and preferences of their fellow teachers, their administrators, and people in general. Role theory implies that role behavior will remain stable and satisfying only so long as congruence exists between the perceived demands of others and the individual's actual behavior. If behavior does not match demands, the person ought to feel out of place, incompetent, or under pressure.

To study this congruence, teachers were asked questions about thirty different behaviors. For example, in one case the teachers were asked to rate themselves on how much watching they did for cheaters, on the following scale:

a great deal of watching   (5)
a lot of watching   (4)
a moderate amount of watching (3)
a slight amount of watching   (2)
little or no watching   (1)

The teachers were also asked what they thought people in general would like them to do about cheaters, what school officials would like them to do, and what other teachers would like them to do. The average of their answers is shown in Fig. 1. As can be seen from the figure, teachers report that others, whether teachers, school administrators, or people in general, think they should do a lot of watching for cheaters during a classroom test. Teachers also report they do more than a moderate amount of watching. Since there is considerable congruence between perceived demands and behavior, a role explanation of teacher performance seems appropriate: that is, teachers seem to do what they think others want them to do in this case.

However, role theory implies not merely that *perceived* demands influence performance but also that the *actual* demands (preferences, norms) of relevant others will influence performance. Biddle and his associates also asked school officials, parents, and pupils to state their own expectations and preferences regarding teacher behavior. In contrast to the demands of others as teachers perceive them, shown in Fig. 1, Fig. 2 shows an average of the actual wishes of others in relation to teacher behavior.

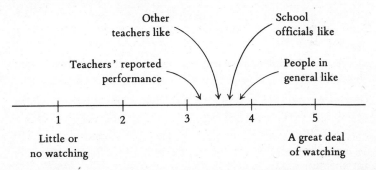

FIG. 1. The average of reports by teachers of "watching for cheaters on a classroom test" and the average of teacher estimates of what others would like them to do.

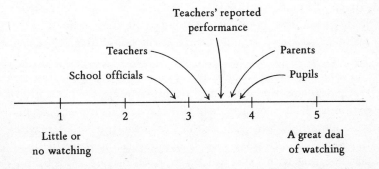

FIG. 2. The average reports by teachers of "watching for cheaters on a classroom test" and the average description by each group of what they would like teachers to do.

The teachers' report of their actual behavior matches closely what other teachers would like them to do. The performance described falls between that preferred by school officials (a moderate amount of watching for cheaters) and that preferred by parents and pupils (a lot of watching). Thus, while the school administrators show clear disagreement with parents and pupils, the teachers differ by a smaller amount from each of them. This fits the role model well. If the teachers' behavior were completely in agreement with the expectations of one group, they would be faced by considerable concern from the other group.

A third assumption of role theory is that those holding a position can accurately perceive the role demands held by others. Comparing Figs. 1 and 2, we note that teachers do pretty well in estimating how other teachers and people in general want them to behave but do poorly in estimating the desires of school officials. They assume school officials want them to do substantially more watching for cheaters than school officials actually report wanting. If role theory is correct and teachers' performance is influenced by their perception of school administrators' desires, giving teachers a more accurate view of these desires should reduce the effort spent in watching for cheaters.

In general, studies of this type have been concerned with the lack of congruence among desires actually held by different groups. Twyman and Biddle (1963) present some interesting findings on this point. Parents indicated they wanted more maintenance of order and control in the school (e.g., "keeping students quiet in the library," "supervising on the playground," "threatening pupils misbehaving in the classroom") than did the teachers themselves. Parents also desired more teacher participation in PTA meetings than did teachers. However, parents were more indulgent with teachers than the teachers were with themselves for "reading own books during the study period" and "visiting with other teachers on the playground." School officials agreed more with teachers on appropriate teacher behavior than did parents, while pupils desired the greatest self-indulgence from teachers of any group. As far as pupils were concerned, teachers could spend much of their time in school talking with one another, preparing assignments, and grading exams rather than supervising pupils or in direct teaching. Pupils varied in their desires for teacher maintenance of order and control, depending on the specific situation; sometimes they wanted less control (e.g., less "keeping pupils quiet in the library"), and sometimes they wanted more control ("threatening pupils misbehaving in the classroom").

What do these findings mean? For one thing, they suggest that there is not a homogeneous societal conception of the teacher's role. Pupils, parents, teachers, and school administrators do not wholly agree with one another on what is appropriate behavior for teachers. This might suggest some ambiguity or conflict in carrying out the role. If a teacher tries to behave as others wish him to act but others disagree on their demands, the teacher is faced with a dilemma. However, the results of Twyman and Biddle's study also indicate that the greatest degree of agreement exists between teachers and those who have the most direct control over them, namely, school administrators. This would tend to reduce tension in performing the teacher role, since those who can control the most effective rewards and punishments for the teacher employ the same criteria for adequate role performance as the teacher himself. This agreement is probably facilitated by the fact that school administrators have almost all been teachers themselves. The agreement might also be the result of teacher acceptance of administrators' standards in order to survive in the teacher role.

The substantial discrepancies between teacher and pupil expectation are interesting. Ordinarily, the lack of agreement between role partners, i.e., those participating in interacting positions, would lead to role strain or tension. However, the teacher's role is not dependent on student preference. The teacher has a great deal of power to employ sanctions with his pupils who have relatively little power in return. The teacher is primarily at the mercy of his principal and only partially controllable by parents, pupils, and other teachers.

Experimental Role Assignment

We have examined the most common method of investigating roles, which is to ask persons to describe their expectations and wishes regarding the behavior of a person in a particular position. An alternative method is to see what differences in behavior occur when persons are assigned different positions. An investigation by Buckhout and Guskin (1968) illustrates this approach. Some previous work in health education (Guskin and Taylor, 1968) suggests that teachers see their role as a protective one rather than an arousing one. To see whether this hypothesis could be demonstrated in a laboratory situation, college students were asked to make statements to another student about tuberculosis—to *teach* the other person about TB, to *persuade* the other person to take an x-ray, or merely to *express* their own opinions to the listener. They were given a choice of high or low fear statements to use in their communication. The average "persuader" chose twice as many high as low fear statements about TB in trying to "sell" x-rays, whereas the "teachers" and "opinion givers" both chose approximately equal numbers of high and low fear statements. The "persuaders" also had a much higher heart rate during their communication than did the other two groups, who were again similar. It appears that for the students in this situation, "teaching" was a low pressure role involving neither personal arousal nor a willingness to arouse the pupil. If this phenomenon is found more generally it would suggest that teaching is more concerned with avoiding strain than with inducing change. For any major change to occur in the effectiveness of teaching, it may be necessary to change the image of the teacher from that of a protective mother figure to that of an aggressive salesman. This may be what is happening as educators shift from a permissive and adjustment-oriented philosophy to an achievement-oriented philosophy.

Role Conflicts

Another method of studying the teacher role is to focus directly on problem areas. An investigation by Getzels and Guba (1955) identified areas of role conflict and then sought to determine how disturbing each type of conflict was to teachers as well as what the related factors were. Three items from a questionnaire they administered to teachers suggest the sort of conflicts explored.

Although the community expects a teacher to maintain the same standard of living as, say, a minor executive or successful salesman, the salary typically paid a teacher is too small to make this possible.

While almost no one even concerns himself with the conduct of the average individual unless he seriously violates the customs and conventions of the community, many people are constantly on guard to be certain that teachers behave appropriately at all times.

While many parents expect the teacher to discipline their child as well as to educate him, these same parents are often resentful of the disciplinary methods employed, even when those methods are justified.[1]

The investigators found that some of the conflicts explored were prevalent in all the schools they examined, others varied more depending on the school situation, and still others occurred only in a few schools. The degree of disturbance felt in each area of potential role conflict differed from teacher to teacher, with men, as a rule, experiencing greater conflict than women. Some reasons for this sex difference can be suggested. The woman's social and economic status is less likely to be determined by her own income; thus a low income is not a source of role conflict. The restrictions placed on conduct of teachers are prevalent for women in general and not merely for teachers. Finally, for the woman there are fewer occupational alternatives which have higher professional prestige. In short, the differences in role conflict experienced by the male and female teachers in this country are closely related to the

1   J. Getzels and E. Guba, The structure of roles and role conflict in the teaching situation. *Journal of Educational Psychology* 29, 30-40 (1955).

observation that teaching is frequently seen as a female profession and is regarded as a desirable occupation for females and an undesirable or low status occupation for males.

Role Training

Most of what we have discussed thus far concerns the relationship between what others expect and what the teacher does. Yet in our society we do not place a person in a teaching position and then let him guess what others want him to do. We invest a great deal in educational programs to train teachers. Why, then, does this role training so often fail? One answer lies in the failure of training programs to recognize the role demands that will be placed on teachers on the job. The graduate of a teacher training program is evaluated on the job, not by his professors but by administrators in his school. Furthermore, the tasks and situational demands of full-time teaching may not resemble the situation described or experienced in training. Thus a junior high school social studies teacher may be well versed in the latest "discovery" methods for teaching principles of government yet find, if he is hired to teach in an "inner city" school, that he has to cope with students who read at third grade level, who are hostile to school, who fight, challenge the teacher physically, and just plain ignore the usual rules for maintaining order. Under such circumstances, the teacher is going to consider as secondary any techniques for stimulating interest in the subject matter. This is reinforced by the school administrator's evaluation of him in terms of his ability to maintain order. Since his training gave him few resources for dealing with the actual classroom situation he now faces, he seeks out "experienced" teachers who are able to handle (i.e., control) their classes. The old hands give the young recruit the hints necessary for gaining control of the class. In the process he casts aside the modern teaching skills he learned in college and takes on the role behaviors of the experienced teachers. He thus has been retrained to deal with the control problems of the classroom. These control techniques may be a far cry from the procedures recommended in any course in college. Yet if they meet the demands of his present situation and result in positive evaluation by his superiors, they will be considered as appropriate role behavior and maintained.

The tragedy in such situations is that almost no one in the school is prepared to assume an appropriate educational role with the type of pupil encountered. Teachers and administrators are unable to deal with the needs and behaviors of these students because they have initially been socialized[2] into roles which are not relevant to the school conditions they encounter, and so they now feel inadequate to handle the educational process. They develop a feeling of futility and often give up any hope of educating their students; instead they resort to policing the classroom and getting through the day. This resembles a custodial rather than an educational role.

It would seem, then, that if teacher training programs are to cope with the problems critical to the real world of teaching, they cannot ignore the noninstructional demands placed on the teacher, they should simulate the situational and social demands of teaching as realistically as possible during training, and finally they should develop techniques to enable the teacher to assume an appropriate instructional role.

THE ROLE OF THE PUPIL

In discussing the role-determined behavior of the teacher, we have given great emphasis to the part played by others' expectations *for* the teacher. When the pupil role is examined, it is the expectation held *by* the teacher that becomes crucial. The teacher has formal authority over the pupil with all the possibilities for reward and punishment which go with it. He utilizes his power to demand orderly behavior and to motivate academic performance. In general, we think of these role demands as being common to all teacher-pupil relationships. However, there is evidence that teachers may differentially

2   See Chapter 7 for a fuller description of socialization processes.

enforce role demands based on differential expectations about pupil performance.

Expectations about Individual Pupils

In an investigation by Rosenthal and Jacobson (1968a), reported in their book *Pygmalion in the Classroom*, experimenters administered a group intelligence test to all pupils in an elementary school but led teachers to believe that the test was a measure of potential for intellectual "blooming." At the beginning of the school year each of the 18 teachers was told the names of five or six children in his class who, on the basis of test performance, were predicted to show marked intellectual gains during the next few months. Actually, the experimenters drew the names at random from those in the teachers' class. Later in the school year, the tests were readministered and it was found that the randomly chosen "bloomers" had indeed gained more in intellectual performance than their classmates. Although others have since raised serious questions about the research methodology, the experimenters claimed they had demonstrated that changing teacher expectations can have a marked effect on pupil performance. The investigators believed the effect might be explained by subtle aspects of the interaction between a teacher and his pupils.

Her tone of voice, facial expression, touch, and posture may be the means by which—probably quite unwittingly—she communicates her expectations to the pupils. Such communication might help the child by changing his conception of himself, his anticipation of his own behavior, his motivation, or his cognitive skills.[3]

A less subtle way in which teacher expectations may influence pupil performance is demonstrated in an investigation by Beez (1968). In this study, sixty master's-level students in a teacher

---

3   R. Rosenthal and L. Jacobson, Teacher expectations for the disadvantaged. *Scientific American* 218 (4), 19-23 (1968), p. 23. Copyright © 1968 by Scientific American, Inc. All rights reserved.

training program were each asked to tutor a five-year-old disadvantaged child, supposedly so that the experimenter could find out something about the learning characteristics of these children. Before meeting the child, the tutor was given a faked one-page psychological report on the child which indicated, among other things, the psychologist's estimate of the potential of the child for success in school tasks. Half of the tutors were given reports which suggested that the child had high potential and half of the reports indicated that the child had low potential. As in the Rosenthal and Jacobson study, the reports were assigned at random rather than on the basis of any true differences among the children.

The first learning task on which the tutors worked with the children was a word recognition task. The tutor was given twenty cards, each bearing a word such as "men" or "stop," and was told to teach the child as many as he thought he could in ten minutes. An observer recorded the behavior of the teacher, and the child was tested later to see how much he had learned. Teachers who thought the child had high potential covered twice as many words in the time allotted as did those who were informed the child had low potential. The amount of material covered was not influenced by the tutor's previous teaching experience, though this experience ranged from none to twenty years. The result of the differences in teacher performance were clearly reflected in pupil performance. When the "high potential" pupils were tested, they obtained twice as many correct answers as the "low potential" pupils. Pupil performance was little influenced by pupil IQ, which ranged from below 70 to above 120 as measured on a vocabulary test.

The Beez study clearly shows that one way in which a teacher may let his expectations influence pupil performance is by varying the quantity of material covered or the difficulty level of the material. With the low-potential pupil the teacher, in Beez's study, spent his time reviewing the same words and explaining the meaning of words, whereas for the high-potential pupil he covered more words. This is only one way in which a teacher expectation can become a "self-fulfilling prophecy."

Expectations about Groups of Students

The impact of a teacher's expectations upon his definition of the pupil role and resulting pupil performance is important because it may operate not only in isolated instances but for a whole classroom or whole categories of students. The urban ghetto school may be a good case in point. Schoolteaching is a middle-class occupation, and therefore draws to it teachers who either are from the middle class or who aspire to middle-class status and hold middle-class values. They are then trained in middle-class-oriented schools of education. The result is that they expect their students to come dressed and motivated much as their own children would. When they are faced with Negro children who are poorly dressed and who speak a nonstandard dialect of English, they often assume a low ability. They are reinforced in this by intelligence tests which grossly discriminate against nonwhite, nonmiddle-class students (see Pettigrew, 1964). The consequence is that they expect their students to fail and the students do fail.

Students fail and drop out of school for many reasons, but one of the most important seems to be the sense of continual failure and a feeling of hopelessness as a student. It is possible that teachers communicate their own feelings of futility and their low expectations for their students. In a sense, the teachers may be creating a student role which precludes success; the teacher's expectation which the student may internalize is that he is a failure. Kenneth Clark writes in *Dark Ghetto* (1965):

Once one organizes an educational system where children are placed in tracks or where certain judgements about their ability determine what is done for them or how much they are taught or not taught, the horror is that the results seem to justify the assumptions. The use of intelligence test scores to brand children for life, to determine education based upon tracks and homogeneous groupings of children, impose on our public school system an intolerable and undemocratic social hierarchy, and defeat the initial purposes of public education. They induce and perpetuate the very pathology which they claim to remedy.

Children who are treated as if they are uneducable almost invariably become uneducable.[4]

The pupil is not only under the strong influence of the teacher but also very much under the control of other pupils and of his parents. Since teachers, pupils, and parents often value different behaviors, students may frequently find themselves in a predicament. The teacher in the classroom may demand that students be quiet, that they prepare their lessons carefully, and that they not cheat. At the same time, fellow students may feel that teasing the teacher is a good thing, that silence is anything but golden, that cheating is desirable, and that doing homework indicates that you are the "teacher's pet."

Such a student is in a conflict situation. Whose demands does he follow—the teacher's or his peers'? If the student refuses to conform to either, he will be punished. If he is quiet and attentive in class, his friends will think he is "polishing the apple." If he is "one of the boys" and makes a lot of noise and is unprepared, the teacher will punish him.

Certainly, role conflict or role tension is not limited to pupils. We have seen it among teachers and it is also common among school superintendents.

THE ROLE OF THE SCHOOL ADMINISTRATOR

A study by Gross, Mason, and McEachern (1957) of school system superintendents indicates that they are frequently faced with conflicting demands from the school board, their teachers, and their own expectations of the role of superintendent. On the issue of teacher salary, for example, the school board is likely to want to hold down costs by keeping salaries low, while the teachers want a salary which is appropriate for their professional status. The superintendent would like to have

---

4   K. B. Clark, *Dark Ghetto: Dilemmas of Social Power.* New York: Harper & Row, 1965. Quoted by permission of the publisher.

salaries high so he can keep and recruit fine teachers. What does the superintendent do in such a situation? While he would like the good will of the teachers, he is dependent upon the school board if he wishes to maintain his position. In their study Gross, Mason, and McEachern found that different superintendents resolved these conflicting demands in different ways:

There were "moralists" who made their decision on the basis of what they felt to be right, regardless of how much they might be punished by a pressure group in the community;

There were "expedients" who made their decision on the basis of how much they would gain or lose in support by making the decision; and

There were "moral-expedients" who weighed each of these two approaches in some balanced manner.

Moralists were, in a sense, rejecting the momentary pressures of the situation, while the expedients tended to be much more concerned with them. This does not mean, however, that the moralists were rejecting the role of the superintendent. Role behaviors are not only the result of momentary pressures but also are the result of rules, regulations, and expectations of others (as well as of organizations) which are learned and internalized. When we speak of the role of the superintendent, we are referring to a learned set of behaviors acquired over a long period of time, and internalized to the extent that the individual will behave as a superintendent, whether or not others in his immediate environment apply pressure on him to do so.

In a sense, roles important to an individual (e.g., role of husband or wife) become part of his image of himself—not to act in a manner consistent with such a role means that an individual is acting contrary to his own expectations for himself. This is one of the major reasons for the debilitating effects of role conflict; the individual is being forced to act in two contradictory roles, both of which *he* feels he should perform.

Thus far, role problems and conflicts have been categorized by the type of person involved—teacher, pupil or administrator. The sources of conflict associated with roles may be categorized in the following manner:

a) disagreement in role expectations between the person in the role and important other persons, e.g., self and boss;

b) disagreement in role expectations between two other important persons or groups, e.g., one's parents and teachers in regard to the role of student;

c) conflict in demands from important others for two overlapping roles, e.g., parents' expectations for the role of a child who helps with business and teachers' expectations for the role of a student who should study and be active in extracurricular activities;

d) inconsistencies in expectations held by another person or group, e.g., a mother wants her son to act as an independent adult and a dependent child;

e) incompatibility between personal style and role expectations, e.g., an effeminate man in the role of physical education teacher;

f) incompatibility of role expectations with reality demands or possibilities, e.g., the role of administrator which requires an extensive array of abilities and a 28-hour work day.[5]

CONCLUSION

Role theory enables us to look beyond the particular personality of the individual student or teacher and see that people, to a great extent, behave the way they do as a result of the social situations within which they live and work. Individuals bring with them to any particular situation a history of

---

5   For a review of the concept of role conflict see Secord and Backman, 1964, and Brim, 1966.

past successes and failures and feelings of adequacy or inadequacy, not necessarily the result of certain basic personality types but often the result of the pressures and expectations to which they have been and are subjected. These forces often are built into the organizations within which they work and play. There are certain requirements which they are expected to follow; to reject them sets in motion sanctions which attempt to force compliance. Similarly, other people in the situation—with or without overt sources of punishment—expect them to behave in certain ways. Again, if they fail to live up to these expectations there will be an attempt to pressure them to change their behavior so that it conforms with the desired performance.

A major asset of viewing behavior from a role-theory perspective is that behavior can be seen as alterable. The teacher who expects a student to fail and unintentionally rewards failure can alter the student's behavior if he recognizes the influence of his own expectations and changes them. On the other hand, if the teacher assumes that the student's performance is a function of "flaws" in pupil personality, convincing the teacher to change is extremely difficult or impossible.

This is not to say that a student's perception of his own role as learner can be rapidly changed by a prior change in his teacher's orientation. Rather, it emphasizes that change is feasible. It also emphasizes that teachers who are taught and encouraged to have certain role expectations for students can be trained differently so that they have the competency, the desire, and the hope to teach their students.

CHAPTER TWO

TEACHER AND PUPIL PERCEPTIONS OF ONE ANOTHER

In Chapter 1 we discussed social behavior in terms of role theory. Another vantage point from which social behavior may be examined is that of person perception or interpersonal perception—i.e., the way people look at, and evaluate, one another. The central concerns of research on person perception are (1) to determine how people come to "understand" or form impressions of one another, and (2) to determine how this understanding is related to other interpersonal skills and behavior.

Let us apply the person perception approach to the earlier illustration of an aggressive teacher's response to the rebellious behavior of a seventh grader. A person perception analysis might note that the boy perceived that the teacher was a "softie," somebody who could be pushed around. The teacher, in turn, perceived that the student was really weak and would be submissive to an aggressive autocratic approach. The pupil's perception was inaccurate, and resulted in an ineffective action which led to a frightening experience for him. In the future, he would perceive the teacher as strong and probably conform to the teacher's requests, which would result in a more satisfactory adjustment for him. The teacher's perception was accurate, and led to effective behavior which prevented a further occurrence of the tense interaction.

ACCURACY OF PERSON PERCEPTION

There would be great value in the person perception approach if we could measure the accuracy of person perception and could demonstrate that some people are consistently accurate, and that this accuracy leads to consistently effective behavior. If the seventh grade teacher was truly a perceptive person, when another student refused to cooperate and cursed him he might accurately note that this boy was quite different, perhaps mentally ill, and that the student might respond to physically aggressive attack by pulling a knife and attempting to kill the teacher. Thus the teacher might ignore the student's insolence or tell the student that he would speak to him later. Role analysis, by itself, would predict the same teacher behavior with both pupils.

The exciting possibility of being able to identify accurate interpersonal perceivers who would be more effective social beings or, more specifically, more effective psychotherapists, teachers, and parents has led to a great deal of research. A study by Gage, Leavitt, and Stone (1955) investigated the widely held proposition that teachers should understand their pupils. More specifically, they asked whether the accuracy with which a teacher perceived cognitive, social, and emotional characteristics of his pupils bore any relationship to the effectiveness of a teacher's behavior as judged by his pupils. In the cognitive area, they assumed that a teacher would teach better if he could accurately evaluate the competence of his pupils, where they stood in understanding of the material presented, and whether they were ready for the next task. To determine teacher accuracy in this area, the experimenters gave 103 fourth through sixth grade teachers pairs of items from standardized achievement tests and asked the teachers to identify which of each pair of items would be harder for pupils. Unfortunately, teacher accuracy in answering these questions bore little relationship to pupils' evaluations of how well their teacher explained things to them.

Since teachers are expected to foster social adjustment in pupils, it was assumed that they should be aware of pupils' social status in the classroom. They should know who likes whom and who is most and least popular. Teachers did show substantial, though nowhere near perfect, accuracy in predicting pupils' preferences. Unfortunately again, there was little relationship between this accuracy and the social adjustment of their pupils.

Finally, it was assumed that a good teacher should understand his pupils' personal problems. Teachers were asked to guess how four of their pupils would answer a problem inventory ("Which of these two problems worries you most?"). Teachers performed only slightly better than they would have by blind guessing. Furthermore, those who performed better were not seen by pupils as coping better with pupil problems.

This study indicated that teachers are often highly inaccurate in understanding their pupils and that when they are accurate in perceiving cognitive characteristics, i.e., achievement, they are not accurate in perceiving social and personality characteristics, and vice versa. Most important of all, the study failed to provide any evidence that those who perceive or understand pupils better are actually better teachers.

Where does this leave us? One study in itself is not conclusive but many studies have been carried out on this and similar questions with similar results (e.g., Cline, 1964). Accuracy in understanding or perceiving others on one characteristic is not closely related to accuracy in judging other characteristics. Nor does accuracy seem to be related to good performance on the job.

How is it possible that accuracy in perceiving pupil characteristics is unrelated to the effectiveness of teacher behavior?

For one thing, despite the great emphasis in the educational literature on individualizing instruction, teaching a classroom of 30 children allows little opportunity for true individualization of teaching. A teacher may as well perceive his students as similar to one another since he must treat them as a unit. Second, a teacher may need to respond only to the momentary feelings and learning problems of his pupils and not to any underlying stable characteristics of the children. He doesn't need to know whether this class finds math easy or difficult, but only whether they can do this problem he is giving them now.

Perhaps what is most important is how the teacher reacts to such information when it is received. When a child does poorly, does the teacher simply say to himself, "He's stupid—I won't bother with him"; or does he change his pace for the child or give him special attention? In the area of social and personal problems, again, the most serious problems are probably noticed by most teachers, but how they cope with the situation may differ considerably given the same "understanding." Furthermore, teachers who fail to understand their pupils' problems may help them anyway, simply because they like children or encourage everyone to participate or don't overreact to the unnoticed problem. In short, there has been too great a focus on whether a person is or is not sensitive rather than on what a person needs to be sensitive to, especially in the classroom setting.

Perhaps the most important teacher perceptions of pupils are those which deal with the competence either of individual students or of the class as a whole in a particular skill or content area and with the reactions of pupils to the teacher's presentations and assignments. The evaluation of student readiness, attention, boredom, and attainment are required for effective structuring of learning tasks. While standardized tests can be of some help and teacher-made tests can fill much of the gap in teacher information about student progress, the inability to pick up continuous cues from students is a serious hindrance to effective teaching and learning. This should be very obvious, since all of us have had to sit through too many tedious, uninformative lectures and to carry out too many assignments for which teachers had given inadequate instructions. However, it should be clear that while teacher and pupil perceptions of one another may have considerable impact on school learning, it is probably not a general "understanding" teachers have or do not have of students which makes for effective teaching. Rather, such effectiveness is probably a result of the accuracy of the *specific momentary assumptions* that teachers make about how students will interact with them and what learning experiences pupils are ready to respond to.

INDIVIDUAL DIFFERENCES IN PERCEPTION

We have seen that the investigations of individual's perceptiveness have not been very fruitful. Yet there are differences among people in how they perceive others. Two important factors which lead to such differences are (1) our motivational state, i.e., our desires, needs, wishes, and values; and (2) our perceptual style, i.e., how we tend to organize what we see. If two people look at the same vague picture and one says it is two men in a contest and the other says it is two long-parted friends embracing, the two viewers probably differ in their fears, problems, and needs. This principle lies behind some very popular devices for personality evaluation known as projective techniques—procedures based on the assumption that a person will "project" his internal images, wishes, and needs upon an external stimulus, such as a picture. If a person responded to several pictures with stories about men striving for success, he might be judged to have a high need for achievement. If the second person responded with several stories about people seeking one another out, he might be judged to have a high need for affiliation.

The pictures employed on these tests are intentionally ambiguous to facilitate projection rather than accuracy. A natural situation like a classroom contains unambiguous as well as ambiguous stimuli. But there certainly is considerable room for misperception. Did that child give the wrong answer because he mis-heard the question or because he wasn't prepared? Is that Negro boy who seems to be holding that white girl's hand being "fresh" or is he returning something she dropped? Are those students passing notes to make fun of the teacher or trying to pass on an important message without disturbing the class? Are they laughing with me or against me? Do they really understand what I'm saying or are they just nodding their heads to seem knowledgeable? It is easy to see that teachers may differ considerably in how ready they are to choose one or the other interpretation in these situations. Some are more ready to see the student as competent, honest, friendly, and responsible; others are more ready to see the student as inadequate, fresh, impertinent, and stupid. Of course, pupils' perceptions of teachers may be similarly distorted by their own needs. A Negro student who has felt degraded in his past experiences with white adults may be ready to interpret a white teacher's correction of his reading as a slur rather than a piece of useful information.

Individuals differ not only in the needs they project onto their social world but also in the degree and type of organization of their experience. Some people respond to minute details, others to the total pattern of their environment. Some see the social world as simple, others as complex. Some react impulsively, others reflectively. Certain of these differences in style have been explored by projective techniques such as the Rorschach inkblot test, where the blots may be responded to as a whole, or in part, slowly or quickly, in an organized or disorganized fashion, with attention to form or to shading. Consistency in such responses is held to be related to more general personality styles. Other differences in style have been explored more recently in extensive research efforts. For example, Witkin and his associates (1954) have investigated what they call "field dependence," that is, the extent to which a person can separate items from a distracting background. In one of Witkin's perceptual experiments, subjects are placed in a tilted adjustable chair in a tilted room and asked to adjust the chair until they are sitting upright. Field-dependent persons do very poorly on this task, being influenced so much by the tilted visual field (the room) that they often consider themselves upright when they are tilted 20° from the vertical. Such field-dependent individuals not only depend heavily on visual frameworks but also have been shown to be more easily influenced by group pressures toward conformity (Linton, 1955); they are more likely to perceive the social context than to focus on the essentials of the task. A field-dependent teacher or pupil might overreact to distracting components in the classroom and lose sight of the essential teaching or learning task. The teacher or pupil might be more concerned with how others evaluate him than with what he needs to do to teach or learn the lesson.

Kagan and his coworkers (1965) have identified in children a trait they term "conceptual tempo," which ranges from an impulsive to a reflective style of response to cognitive tasks. The impulsive child does not reflect enough, for example, before naming words when he is learning to read. The result is greater inaccuracy on tasks which require careful discrimination. It is possible that he may also get into trouble because he responds to anticipated instructions from the teacher rather than listening carefully to the teacher's statements.

Another perceptual distinction with social relevance is Frenkel-Brunswik's (1949) "intolerance of ambiguity," a tendency to see ambiguous events in "black or white" terms. Such intolerance of ambiguity has been found to be related to authoritarian attitudes and prejudice. In the classroom this may show itself in a pupil's wanting to decide immediately whether the teacher is for him or against him.

One final characteristic which should be treated here is the simplicity or complexity of an individual's perception of other people. The work of George Kelly (1955) and his students on the way people conceptualize the important people in their life has shown us that some persons see all people as differing only in how good or bad they are. For example, if they like a person they see him as intelligent, attractive, competent, and pleasant; if they dislike him he is seen as stupid, unattractive, etc. In contrast, other persons have much more complex views of people. They may see their best friend as being pleasant but only average in intelligence, while they may see a disliked person as brighter and more attractive but less pleasant than their best friend. Whereas the simple perceiver may see his best friend as differing in every way from a disliked person, the more complex perceiver sees them as similar in some ways and different in others.

It would be interesting to apply this approach to teachers, asking them to compare their students with one another and with themselves. Some teachers might see all the "good" students as similar to one another and to the teacher, having all the "good" traits, and different from all the "bad" students. The "bad" students would be seen as very similar to one another and having all the "bad" traits. Another teacher might make fine discriminations among his students, recognizing that some students who are similar in terms of academic competence are very different in terms of personal tempo, popularity, and leadership qualities. Furthermore, the teacher might note that some of the students with considerable academic and social problems in school nevertheless resemble the teacher in activity level and preference for creative tasks. It would be clear from such descriptions that we were dealing with two very different persons who should have distinctly different ways of teaching. Our first guess might be that the more discriminating teacher would be more effective since he would be better able to handle individual differences in the classroom situation. Although earlier research was discouraging, a study by Flanders (1960) does support this relationship to some extent. Another guess, unsupported by research, is that the discriminating teacher would be ineffective in dealing with the class as a group and too sympathetic with problem children to cope with discipline problems. A third possibility, argued by the work of Thelen (1967) is that there is some ideal match between teacher and child characteristics which fosters effective teaching and that teachers can distinguish which pupils are teachable by them.

We have given considerable attention to individual differences in person perception. Although persons do differ in the way they perceive the social world, it is a mistake to emphasize only the uniqueness of perceivers. There is much research to demonstrate that most people respond to certain social stimuli or social cues in similar ways. One factor explored has been the way initial information influences the first impression we form of other people. In one investigation (Kelley, 1965), college students in their regular psychology classrooms were presented with some biographical material about a substitute instructor just prior to his entering and leading a discussion. The biographical information was a typewritten note distributed individually to students indicating that the instructor was a graduate student with previous college teaching experience but had never taught the course before. After describing his age and marital status, half of the students were given the information that "people who know him consider him to be a rather cold person, industrious, critical, practical, and determined." The other half of the students had the words "rather cold" replaced with "very warm". After the twenty-minute discussion period with the new instructor, all students were asked to give their impressions of the teacher.

Those students to whom the teacher had been initially described as "cold" later rated the teacher as more self-centered, formal, unsociable, unpopular, irritable, humorless, and ruthless; while those students who were given the description with "warm" in it described the teacher as more considerate, informal, sociable, popular, good-natured, humorous, and humane. Not only were the students' impressions influenced by the "warm" versus "cold" information, but the actual behavior with the teacher was influenced by the description the students had been given. Participation in discussion was greater among those who were told the instructor was warm, and those who participated more frequently had the most favorable impression of the instructor.

Here we have a perceptual phenomenon which would seem to have considerable impact on school learning. Certainly, in the natural teaching situation there are many pieces of prior information which students have about their new teachers. This investigation suggests that the initial student perception of the teacher and initial student behavior might be heavily influenced by such information. However, further studies have shown that other adjectives do not have such an effect. Also, the typical teacher will be observed by a student over a considerable length of time, and we would expect the initial impression to be modified if it were inconsistent with the teacher's actual performance. There is, nevertheless, the distinct possibility that a student with an initially negative impression of a teacher would, as a result of his avoidance of interaction with the teacher, fail to expose himself to more positive qualities of the teacher.

Another way of saying this is that negative expectations developed in early phases of a relationship may lead an individual to withdraw from interacting with others, or to distort information which is contradictory to the first impression. This withdrawal and/or distortion results in a continual building up of negative impressions of the other—without any necessary confirmation by the other person. In time, one or both partners in the relationship may have built up, in an autistic (i.e., self-centered and unrealistic) manner, hostile reactions to each other. Thus early expectations are maintained and further interactions are interpreted so as to reinforce these expectations. Newcomb (1947) has referred to this process as "autistic hostility."

The influence of early impressions on later reactions is even more likely to affect the teacher who gets initial information about a student from other teachers, from IQ scores in the student's folder, or from social cues such as the clothing, name, color, or dialect of the pupil. It seems possible that the teacher's first impressions of the student will be more lasting than the pupil's first impression of his teacher, since the teacher is less likely to observe a child with whom he is not interacting, whereas the pupil can observe the teacher interacting with others. The study of teacher expectations of pupil "blooming" (Rosenthal and Jacobson, 1968), described in the last chapter, is an illustration of this effect of first impressions upon the learning process. In that study, prior information about pupil potential affected pupil performance only in the first two grades. One interpretation of the ineffectiveness of the information in the later grades was that students develop reputations, and teacher perceptions and expectations would probably be more responsive to the child's school reputation than to the information provided by an experimenter. Another indication of the potentially damaging effect of a teacher's early impression is the study of tutor-pupil interaction (Beez, 1968), also reported earlier. The pupil is encouraged by the teacher, as a result of the teacher's first impression of the pupil based on a psychological report, to move quickly or slowly through a learning task. Because of the teacher's actions toward the student it is very difficult for progress contrary to his early impressions to occur; that is, a student who is provided more material learns more material and one who is presented less material learns less. In a sense, the teacher may have created a self-fulfilling prophecy.

STEREOTYPES

One kind of prior information which has been extensively examined is the stereotype—any preconception held about members of a particular group or social category. The teacher's response to social cues such as Jewish names, Negroid features, or ragged clothing would be illustrations of response to group membership cues. The significance of the stereotype or preconception is usually held to lie in its unresponsiveness to characteristics of individual members of the stereotyped group. That is, we respond to the "image in our heads" (Lippmann, 1922) rather than to the real characteristics of the person. The teacher reacts to his Negro student as a "colored boy" rather than as "Johnny." And when he views Johnny as a "colored boy," he begins responding to a stereotype which imputes to the child a whole series of behaviors, attitudes, characteristics, and so on. Unfortunately most investigations of stereotypes do not explore the effect of the preconception on the perception of individuals; instead they merely examine how much people agree on the characteristics of "Negroes," "Jews," etc. In contrast is a study carried out a few years ago on the stereotype of the mentally retarded. College students were asked to give their impressions of a boy and girl they observed in film sequences (Guskin, 1962). Both children were mentally retarded and half of the observers were given this information prior to observing either child. Those who were provided this "label" judged the boy to be more similar to the stereotype of the mentally retarded (e.g., incompetent, clumsy, unintelligent) than the students who had no label. The judgment made of the girl was not influenced by labeling. In the film, the boy demonstrated unusual gait, posture, expression, and speech difficulty. Nevertheless he did not fit neatly into the stereotype of the mentally retarded. For example, although his speech was so impaired as to be hardly understandable, the comments of the teacher who was talking with him indicated that the boy could tell time. His ambiguous characteristics seemed to make him particularly vulnerable to the prior information and stereotyping. The girl, on the other hand, displayed few signs of retardation in a first silent segment of film, but showed very clear lag in language and conceptual development when talking to the teacher in the segment with sound. The result was that those with labeling information distrusted it initially because the girl did not present corroborating cues. Later, when the cues were present, the observers realized the relevance of the label. But those who had not received such a label were also able to recognize the clear-cut set of cues to the girl's retardation, in the second segment. As a result, both those with and without the label responded in the same way. Thus this study seems to show that labels and stereotypes can have an important impact on perception when more reliable information is absent but tend to have little significance when more directly observable and relevant cues are present.

The villain, then, seems to be the lack of relevant information rather than the stereotype itself. Similar findings exist in the area of national stereotypes, where we can see the importance of cross-cultural experiences in changing our images of other nations and peoples. Not too many years ago the Russian people were seen as horrible ogres; now it is often said that our problem is more with the leadership of Russia than with its people. Probably the main reasons for this change are twofold; first, the enormously increasing travel—private, governmental, cultural—between the two countries. Numerous Americans have seen Russians and realized they don't have horns. Second, the space race has greatly increased our respect for the scientific capabilities of the Russians, thereby bringing into question the validity of the stereotype of Russia as a technologically backward nation.

We are now in a position to state that stereotypes are not the images held by evil people attempting to force their prejudices on other innocent persons. Rather, stereotypes are the result of a shortage of information resulting from a lack of meaningful contact or the absence of knowledge, combined with man's need to understand the environment in which he lives. Stereotypes are one attempt to order the infinite number of acts performed by the large number of individuals with whom a man has contact. On the basis of some common distinctive trait or label, a class or category of persons is identified. This ordering process can be described as a form of categorization of environmental events. Attributes are assigned to the class, category, or group on the basis of initially available knowledge, whether fact or fancy. This can be called a form of conceptualization. As more and more information is gained about the characteristics and behavior of others, the stereotype or concept attached to the category of persons becomes more and more complex and usually, though not always, more accurate. It may be that when our interaction with another individual provides us with a great deal of information we cease to view him as a member of a particular category but rather as a unique person—much as we view ourselves.

Unfortunately, in categorizing people and in conceptualizing groups so as to enable us to order our environment, if we view groups as different we also often see them in a negative light. This negative image tends to limit contact and/or distort information which is contradictory to the image. When negative images or stereotypes are supported by societal institutions or norms, the result is usually discrimination against the other group.

Prejudice can be said to exist when an individual has a negative stereotype and negative attitude toward a particular group of people. It should be added that prejudice is more often the result of an individual's acceptance of general community attitudes (norms) than a function of his own personality. This was demonstrated in a study by Pettigrew (1958). He administered a measure of authoritarian personality and an anti-Negro questionnaire along with a conformity scale to many people in South Africa and the southern part of the United States. His findings indicated that while a small minority, in both groups, had an authoritarian personality related to prejudicial attitudes and a stereotype of Negroes, the overwhelming majority of those who had a negative, prejudicial attitude toward Negroes were conforming to general societal standards (norms). When these prejudicial norms are held by the teacher as well as community members, the negative consequences for the Negro pupil are obvious.

We have focused primarily on racial stereotypes. What other kinds of stereotypes are most likely to affect teaching? First of all, the stereotype of teachers held by college students is very likely to influence the students' interest in teaching as a career. If elementary school teachers are seen as motherly females, this field is not likely to appeal either to men or to achievement-oriented women. If high school art teachers are seen as persons who aspired to be artists but didn't have the talent to make it, the young art student will not be likely to think of art education as a desirable field.

Once an individual has entered the teaching profession, the stereotypes held by the students, fellow teachers, and the public-at-large may shape the teacher's own concept. If teachers are thought to be overpaid babysitters, the teacher is likely to have a low self-esteem. The teacher may even internalize the image to the extent that he begins to perceive his role as a maternal one. The effect of such internalization and acting out of stereotypes and role expectations may be a permanent change in the individual's behavioral style. Thus it seems that stereotypes held *about* teachers may affect what goes on in the school as much as stereotypes held *by* teachers.

COMMON SENSE PERSONALITY THEORY

Our perceptions of others are not influenced solely by first impressions and stereotypes. One social psychologist (Heider, 1958) has proposed that our perceptions are based on a naive psychology or common sense personality theory. We are not satisfied to perceive the surface behavior of other persons; but seek to go beyond this to perceive the causes and relationships among events and behaviors. We may assume that there were certain abilities, intentions, and a social context which caused the behavior. The individual seeks out the "invariant" characteristics of the person and the situation that will enable him to understand the numerous specific, changing events which he perceives. He seeks to order the world around him so that he can understand it and know how to react to the behavior of the other person. It should be noted that the tendency and need to attribute motivational characteristics to others is especially important when behaviors seem inconsistent. By an attribution of such motivational or personality characteristics, the inconsistencies are "resolved" and understood and this then enables the perceiver to know how he should interact with the other person. Thus, whether the teacher perceives a child who fails to answer as incompetent, unmotivated, or poorly taught will depend on prior observations of the child and knowledge of the current situation. The consequences of these perceptions of causality for teacher behavior might be considerable. It is of critical importance whether these determinants are seen as emanating from the person being viewed or from the environment in which the behavior takes place. If they are seen as a result of factors occurring within the individual, then the behavior is attributed to personality, ability, or motivational factors; if they are seen as a result of the environment, then the behavior is attributed to role demands or social conditions.

In an interesting study by Johnson, Feigenbaum, and Weiby (1964) teachers were led to believe that students initially performed well or poorly. They attributed this initial performance to the individuals. When, on a second learning task, the teachers were led to think the low performers had improved, they attributed this improvement to their own teaching ability. When no improvement was shown, they attributed this to the students' lack of effort and ability. We can apply naive or common sense psychology to the teacher's perception of his Negro student. Many teachers, and people in general, state that the major problem with lower-class Negroes is their lack of ability or motivation, that if they were bright enough or really tried hard enough they could rise above their poverty. On the other hand, a number, unfortunately too few, view the plight of the Negro American as a result of years of discrimination, poor living conditions, miserable schooling, and poor job opportunities. This group views the lower-class Negro child as being subject to enormous environmental pressures which cause his failure. He is seen as being relatively helpless against these pressures, and therefore is not perceived as responsible for his actions. The first group views the problems of Negro students as not being the result of environmental pressures, hence they attribute failure to a lack of ability or motivation within the individuals.

The implications of these two ways of attributing invariant characteristics to the conditions of the lower-class Negro student are of great import for any attempt to change this tendency to fail. If we attribute failure to environmental factors, then we are likely to see our main task as changing the social conditions in which the students live, the structure of the school system to enable it to adjust to the needs of the students, and the training of teachers so that they themselves do not expect the children to fail and force such failure through their teaching methods. On the other hand, if we attribute school failure to a lack of ability or motivation, we are stating that the situation is hopeless or that the pupil is at fault. We demand that the individual improve his effort. In effect, this approach places the real burden on the student, not the society.

CONCLUSION

This discussion further amplifies a point on educational roles made in Chapter 1. It indicates how a perceiver can be led to attribute the cause for a particular kind of behavior to the personality of an individual or to the role pressures to which he is subject. A value judgment of the authors is that the causes for behavior should first be sought in the role requirements and expectations present in particular situations. Personality or motivational factors should be considered only if such role analyses are inadequate to explain the individual's behavior. There is some evidence that this is a "natural" approach to person perception. Jones, Davies, and Gergen (1961) showed that people attribute behavior to another's personality only when he is not behaving consistently with role expectations. In this study the role demands were made very obvious to the viewer. Unfortunately, we are usually relatively ignorant about the variety of role demands facing the other person. Under such conditions, it seems, people are much too prone to look at individuals as separate beings and not as part of very complex social settings.

CHAPTER THREE

THE INTERPERSONAL NATURE OF LEARNING

When we observe what goes on in school, we find teaching carried out by way of social interaction between teachers and students. Is this interaction required for school learning, or is the interaction between teacher and pupil a vestige of an ancient inefficient approach to teaching and learning?

MECHANICAL TEACHERS

The oral, face-to-face approach preceded the printing press, which is now over three hundred years old, yet teachers still lecture as if books didn't exist. The teaching machine is about twenty years old and is hardly used at all. If the book, the teaching machine, and its new relative, computer-assisted instruction, finally take over major teaching responsibilities, it would seem to indicate that an interpersonal view of the learning process will be outdated. The book, teaching machine, and computer-assisted instruction certainly seem to be non-social, impersonal means of teaching and learning; at least they seem so if we think of an interpersonal situation as requiring two or more persons to be visibly present in face-to-face contact. However, if we consider any verbal interchange to be a social encounter, these devices may each be conceived of as merely an efficient way for one or more excellent teachers to interact verbally with many students.

Perhaps this seems too loose a definition of interaction. Reading a book may resemble listening, but not interacting—or does it? Doesn't a good textbook require active participation on the student's part? Notice the use of questions in the last two sentences to get you to respond. The employment of this device illustrates that there is often a kind of dialogue between the writer of the book and the audience. The writer is anticipating the audience and its response to his points. The reader stops to think of responses to the points the writer has raised. To the extent that this interaction is inhibited, the learning of the material is probably impeded. The text seems to have to simulate social interaction to be effective as a teaching tool.

Certainly the teaching machine is mechanical, unsocial. Its very advantage seems to be that it doesn't have the inefficient properties of human interaction. Yet, as with the textbook, its great asset is that its material may be prepared by expert teachers. A teaching machine with a poor program has no value. As a matter of fact the term "teaching machine" has fallen largely into disuse and has been replaced by "programmed instruction," and the program is more likely to be found between the covers of a book than in a machine. Programmed instruction is superior to the use of standard textbooks only if it has been much more carefully prepared than a text, i.e., if the material has been selected more appropriately and sequentially ordered. But the most distinctive feature of programmed instruction is its use of immediate positive feedback to reinforce learning. Following each brief learning segment, the student is required to answer a question on the immediately preceding material. The material and questions are usually written in such a way that the student will give a correct answer. The program then tells him immediately that he is correct, which reinforces what he has learned. This requirement of pupil response and its follow-up by program response provides a greater degree of simulation of verbal interaction between teacher and pupil than does the textbook. In fact, research on normal classroom interaction has shown that much of what goes on follows this pattern: teacher talks and questions, pupil responds, teacher evaluates (Bellak, 1966). The major advantage of the feedback in programmed instruction over classroom teaching is that each student can progress at his own rate.

Individualization is even greater with computer-assisted instruction, since ideally the computer can evaluate each student response to determine what the most appropriate next step should be for this particular student rather than for students generally. If a student indicates by his choice of answers that he is more advanced, he need not review overly simple material. If he is making one kind of error, only that principle need be reviewed. Thus it resembles tutoring more than classroom teaching. The child has the opportunity to respond frequently and get feedback frequently. A good classroom teacher or text can also do this to some extent, but the ideal for this kind of interaction is probably the tutorial relationship.

As has just been pointed out, most learning—whether by book, teaching machine, computer-assisted instruction, lecture, or tutor—has a substantial interpersonal component. Now we shall explore in greater depth four different interpersonal modes of enhancing learning: (1) *discovery* by the student through his own problem-solving efforts, (2) *exposition* by the teacher of verbal statements to be incorporated by the learner into his own thinking, (3) *reinforcement* by the teacher of appropriate learner behavior, and (4) *imitation* by the learner of behavior demonstrated by the teacher.

"DISCOVERY" APPROACHES

The inquiry or discovery methods (Bruner, 1962, p. 20 ff.) are becoming very popular now, particularly in teaching science and social studies. This approach focuses on learning through student problem-solving. The learner is not told the principles of photosynthesis or laissez-faire economics. He "discovers" these himself and is motivated to continue learning by the intrinsic satisfaction of problem mastery. In one modern math approach (Davis, 1963, 1965) the teacher may give the discovery the pupil's name, e.g., "Johnny's theorem" or "Mary's postulate," and refer to the formula in that manner whenever it comes up in group problem-solving efforts; for example, he would say, "If we take Mary's postulate, as Joan suggests, and we then apply Johnny's theorem, what does that give us?" Although the logic of the discovery approach does not require either teacher-pupil or pupil-pupil interaction, it is clear from this example that the interpersonal component may play an important part in this kind of learning.

This interpersonal component becomes a central part of a variation of the discovery approach called the "instructional game" (Boocock and Coleman, 1966). The instructional game is similar in many ways to such popular commercial games as "Monopoly" and "Big Business" with the exception that the rules, situations, and choices are carefully constructed to simulate the real world and the odds of success are based on established principles or statistical findings. One illustration (Boocock and Coleman, 1966) is a legislative game in which several students play the role of a legislative body. Each legislator is given a set of cards which represent the wishes of his constituency. The legislators have to negotiate with one another to get their own bills passed. The effectiveness with which they do this determines whether they get reelected—the goal of the game. Another game is the Career game, in which participants have to plan the weekly activities of a fictional character with the goal of maximizing present and future satisfaction. When they have made the decisions for a "year," spinners and tables based upon national survey data are used to compute scores for the players representing obtained satisfactions in education, occupation, family life, and leisure.

Presumably, the student is learning how to make decisions based on real data and is simultaneously learning what the principles and odds are "out there." Students enjoy playing the games which take advantage of their natural interests, team play, and competition for rewards. These group-motivating aspects of the instructional game are particularly important. As Boocock and Coleman have pointed out, it is time we tried to harness, rather than poorly compete with, the tremendous involvement which high school and college students have in group or team activities and with action in the real world.

It is no wonder that these student problem-solving approaches have a great deal of appeal. They offer the possibility of taking the boredom out of teaching and learning, and of giving a more creative role to both teacher and learner. Furthermore, these methods teach skills which have general applicability rather than a body of knowledge which will be outdated in a few years by new discoveries. Finally, this approach changes the teacher-pupil relationship from an authoritarian one to a more egalitarian or democratic one. The teacher assists the pupils as they cope with the problem together. The student does not have to be told he is "right" by the instructor. The evaluation of the pupil is built into the game as a natural outcome of a successful performance. The instructor has the role of a strategic or tactical consultant.

Despite the appeal of these participation or problem-solving methods, it has been argued that they have certain inherent limitations, the greatest being ineffectiveness and inefficiency in attaining certain goals (Ausubel, 1963). Unless the material is carefully programmed or controlled by the teacher so that there is little chance of error in problem solution, the student is likely to get off on "dead ends," make strategic errors, or come up with the wrong solution. These occurrences may not only slow down learning but also increase the learning of erroneous techniques and content. Yet, if the probability of error is reduced by programming or teacher control, the technique is less likely to have the unique, self-directed, creative, problem-solving character which justifies it. Furthermore, the time and cost per pupil is high for these methods.

In general, the opponents of discovery-oriented approaches argue that individual problem-solving is just not an efficient or effective way of transmitting knowledge and skills. If a culture consists of the learnings passed on from generation to generation, then cultural development requires that the new generation absorb the gains of the previous generation efficiently rather than repeating its problem-solving efforts and errors. The transmission of culture involves the internalization of previously obtained insights. Thus, while inquiry or discovery approaches have an important role in motivating students and in training them in creative problem-solving skills, these methods cannot take on the sole responsibility for education.

EXPOSITION

Perhaps we need to examine under what conditions discovery methods are most appropriate. Flanders (1960) reports that indirect or pupil-oriented teaching is less effective than direct teaching where the goal of teaching is very clear (and concrete), whereas indirect teaching is more effective where the goal of teaching and learning is less obvious. The more traditional method of teaching is the expository presentation by the instructor. This has also been termed "receptive" learning, to emphasize the student's role as a receiver of information rather than as an active participant. Ausubel (1963) has pointed out that the expository method of teaching has fallen into disrepute in recent years because it has been confused with teaching by "rote" methods. However, receptive learning can be much more than merely rote learning. Since rote learning requires that the learner repeat the material exactly as the teacher presented it, it is facilitated by keeping the material separate from other knowledge that the person has accumulated and integrated. In contrast, "meaningfulness" of material requires that it become incorporated into the learner's way of thinking about the subject matter. Thus Ausubel maintains that learning is meaningful only to the extent that the material presented either fits into the existing organization of ideas or alters the existing organization.

Compare the rote learning of definitions of Freud's Id, Ego, and Superego with the understanding of the basic Freudian concepts, i.e., inner conflict between acceptable, civilized, and conscious aspects of the self and unconscious, primitive, and unacceptable aspects of self. One can learn the definitions without any impact on understanding of personality dynamics; but to learn the basic principle in a meaningful way requires that one engage in a major battle between one's existing way of thinking and the new knowledge.

When students talk about forgetting all they have learned (by cramming) the day after the final examination, they are telling us that they have been engaging in nonmeaningful rote learning. While teachers often encourage such rote learning when they evaluate a student's learning by how well his description of concepts fits theirs, the best evidence for meaningful learning is the ability to apply the concept to a problem the teacher has not previously discussed.

The expository method has come under heavy attack because it appears at first glance to be an authoritarian mode of teaching, with the teacher in control. Yet, as Ausubel points out, this is unnecessary. The teacher need not require that his words be dogma nor must the listener accept the teacher's ideas without question. For example, we do not consider reading a book as exposing ourselves to an autocratic relationship. What makes an exposition by a teacher or text autocratic is the implicit orientation of the writer that "You must think the way I tell you because I say so." In contrast, the writer or teacher who provides objective evidence for his positions and presents alternative positions seems to be saying, "My word is not enough. You be the judge of the correct position. You participate in deciding on the 'truth.'" Even the instructor who is giving definitions and presenting rules, laws, or theorems without evidence or alternatives may be saying, "Here is a tool to help you in thinking about this problem. Try it out and see how it works." One way of evaluating whether a relationship is autocratic is to ask whether the listener or reader has a choice of accepting the presentation. An emphasis on rote teaching and learning requires an autocratic teacher who accepts only answers which match his original presentation. Meaningful learning involves an implicit active participation by the learner as well as the teacher. The relationship between ideas of learner and teacher may be one of acceptance and rejection, or one of struggle and accommodation.

Some social psychologists would hold that the implicit participation by a student does not change the basically autocratic nature of the exchange. If students have no control over the manner in which teaching and learning occur, then we are dealing with a largely autocratic, nonparticipating relationship. The question remains just how much and what type of active participation on the part of the student is required before he can respond to an expository presentation as "meaningful" and can integrate the new information with his accumulated knowledge. The answer probably depends on how competent the presenter is in diagnosing where the material fits in relation to the student's current understanding as well as the ability of the presenter to organize the material to mesh with these existing concepts.

REINFORCEMENT APPROACH

An approach which is becoming more commonly used in educational settings is the operant or reinforcement method. The reinforcement method is based on the popular current behaviorist psychology of B. F. Skinner (1953), which holds simply that behavior is modified by its consequences and that the way to alter behavior is to provide reinforcements following desired behavior.

In the typical classroom setting, it is generally assumed that the teacher has control over the rewards and punishments to be applied to pupils when they satisfy the requirements he sets. How is it, then, that the teacher is unsuccessful in modifying the behavior of certain children? To be effective, reinforcement must follow immediately upon desirable behavior. In the typical classroom setting, the teacher is unable to systematically observe all the relevant behavior and unable to selectively reinforce appropriate behavior. The teacher usually gives tests periodically—say once a day or week—to evaluate the adequacy of pupil learning, whereas learning is going on continuously. The teaching machine, or programmed instruction, was developed by Skinnerians to give more continuous control over learning through frequent—about once a paragraph—reinforcement of correct responding. Teaching in Skinnerian terms is "shaping" behavior—that is, modifying behavior in gradual steps by reinforcing successive approximations to the desired responses. The instructional program requires that the learner make new responses following exposure to material of increasing difficulty, and it is the responses which are seen to change as a result of reinforcement.

Given that the teacher does not have the control over learning that the teaching machine has, he still provides reinforcements for the pupil's behavior which should modify the responses. Thus volunteering by a pupil can be increased or decreased depending upon teacher response to the raised hand and to the answer given. In short, any action which obtains a response from the teacher comes under his control. The problem is that in a large classroom, few individual pupil behaviors can be observed and responded to. For example, a considerable amount of pupil behavior is internal verbalization (thought). Perhaps the pupil characteristic which requires most reinforcement for effective learning is attentiveness, yet this is most difficult to identify continuously for all pupils. Here, perhaps, is the greatest advantage of the frequent pupil responding and reinforcement required by the teaching machine. The machine demands attention.

One common application of reinforcement procedures ("operant techniques") in the classroom is in the control of deviant behavior or management problems, such as pupils getting out of their seats or talking out of turn. In approaching such a problem, the "precision teacher," as some operant-trained teachers are called, would first identify the specific behavior with which he is concerned and then record how frequently the behavior occurs. Then he would plan the method for changing the behavior, such as removing the child immediately to an isolated area of the room for five minutes every time the inappropriate behavior occurs. The teacher then consistently applies this procedure and records changes in the frequency with which the undesired behavior occurs. If no behavior change occurs, a new strategy is tried.

There is nothing unusual about most of the strategies employed by the precision teacher. All teachers observe pupil behavior and give rewards and punishments for desirable and undesirable behavior. It is the precision with which behavioral principles are applied that is most distinctive.

Reinforcement theory can be applied to pupil control of teacher behavior as well as teacher control over pupil behavior. There is the well-known cartoon of a rat in a "Skinner box" who is pressing a lever to get food and turns to another rat to say, "Boy, have I got that experimenter controlled. Everytime I press this bar, he gives me some food." In fact, how the pupil responds to the teacher must influence what the teacher does. If the class shows inattention and disruptive behavior when the teacher tries out a new way of presenting material, he is not as likely to try it again. If a child continually gives confusing answers when asked questions, the teacher will stop asking him questions. It would be interesting to train pupils to modify teacher behavior in the same way in which the "precision teacher" modifies pupil behavior.

It can be seen that reinforcement theory is a useful way of describing certain aspects of teacher-pupil interaction and provides a framework for constructing effective instructional programs. The question remains whether this is the most fruitful way of conceptualizing human learning and the most efficient model for teaching, planning curriculum, and producing instructional materials.

Until recently, the method of altering behavior most neglected by contemporary psychologists was imitation. Imitation was disavowed as a legitimate concept for years because of its early incorporation into lists of "instincts" which were thought to account for much of social behavior. When the emphasis in psychology shifted from a genetic to an environmental or learning approach, the huge lists of instincts fell into disrepute. Despite the low status that imitation has as a psychological concept, the phenomena it deals with are obviously very important. As a result, psychologists have tried to account for imitative learning using behaviorist principles such as reinforcement theory (Berger and Lambert, 1968). More recent work has shown that while reinforcement may increase the likelihood of an observer's behaving like the model he is watching, merely seeing the behavior is enough to learn it. If a child watches a person kick a dummy and is then placed in a private room with the dummy, he is much more likely to kick the dummy than if he had not seen the dummy kicked (Bandura, 1965). This is true even if the child is not rewarded for kicking, and has not seen the model rewarded for the act. However, the frequency of such acts by the child is increased by reinforcement of either himself or the model.

The potential usefulness of the concept of imitation in school learning is much greater than that of reinforcement since the teacher is more easily able to act as a model for a large number of pupils than to act as selective reinforcer for each of them.

Two types of imitation or modeling behavior should be distinguished: intentional and incidental. The teacher may be an incidental model for middle-class adult behavior for the child; that is, the children may learn how "respectable" adults behave from him, without conscious effort on the part of either the teacher or the children. The teacher also provides intentional models, as when he demonstrates to pupils how they should add fractions by doing it himself at the blackboard. Perhaps the most common instance of overlap between incidental and intentional imitative learning is in language and speech learning. The teacher will frequently present new words intentionally to young children, pronouncing them and illustrating how they can be used in sentences. At the same time, without being conscious of it, he is using many words unfamiliar to the children in relevant contexts and the children may begin using these without having tried to learn them.

Both intentional and incidental imitative learning require attention to the model or actor. A study by Dorothea Ross (1966) has shown that preschool children with greater dependency needs attend to different cues than less dependent children. In this study, children observed an adult model demonstrating a post office game. The model carried out purposive tasks directly related to the game, such as mailing a letter and selling stamps, and irrelevant actions, such as singing a tune and tapping on objects as she passed by. When asked to play the game themselves, the more dependent children carried out a greater proportion of the irrelevant (or incidental) actions than the less dependent children who were more task-oriented. The lesser selectivity of the dependent children suggests a more general tendency to observe others and model their behavior after them.

Though observation of a pattern of behavior may often be enough to *learn* it, other motivating or reinforcing conditions may be required before the behavior is *produced* by the learner. Thus the lower-class child may learn how a middle-class teacher speaks, but he is not likely to speak that way himself since he may be laughed at by his friends and family for doing so. That he can speak in a middle-class manner might be seen if we have the children put on a skit for one another in which the teacher's behavior is mimicked. The mimicked behavior is likely to be a poor imitation but does differ from the child's usual speech. The poor quality of the imitation comes from the lack of practice of the verbal responses.

In other words, observation does not usually give enough information to transform the behavior of the observer into behavior identical to that of the model. This is clear enough to anyone who has tried to play golf or tennis after watching others play. You may be able to swing the club or racket and hit the ball as a result of having watched others, but that's a far cry from playing as well as the people you've been watching.

A distinction should be made between imitation, conformity, and obedience. Imitation, of course, need not involve felt pressure by the observer to change his behavior, whereas in conformity and obedience there is an implied pressure to adapt to powerful demands. Conformity and obedience differ in whether the norms or standards one tries to match are group norms or the norms of an authority figure. In the classroom any child, as well as the teacher, can serve as a model for *imitation;* the clique a child belongs to may place considerable *conformity* pressures on him, and, of course, the teacher places *obedience* demands on the child. The greatest strain on the child probably comes from the conflicting conformity and obedience pressures. If the learner is faced merely with two discrepant models, neither of whom have great power over him, then the conflict is minor. However, if both models are powerful, the conflict can be very debilitating. Perhaps the most fruitful way to conceive of conformity and obedience is as specialized cases of imitation where considerable negative sanctions can be invoked if modeling does not occur, the sanctions deriving from a peer group in one case and an authority figure in the other. Here we refer again to Ausubel's notion that receptive learning is not necessarily authoritarian. It becomes so when obedience to behavior models is strongly enforced by invoking sanctions.

When we think of "obedience" we do not usually imagine an authority figure, such as a teacher, demonstrating appropriate behavior and then requiring that it be modeled. Usually the teacher tells children what they should do and expects them to be able to do it. If the behavior is in their repertoire of responses, this direct control over persons through instructions and commands is an extremely efficient way to teach. The students need only learn which combination of responses already mastered are now appropriate for this task. If they do not have these responses already in their repertoire, then this expository method becomes quite ineffective.

CONCLUSION

Most teaching and learning involves some combination of the four interpersonal modes we have discussed. For new behavior to be taught, the most efficient procedure seems to be to instruct the person verbally as to what skills he can use, to demonstrate those behaviors which are either not already available to the learner or which are not easily verbalized, and to have him try to perform the behavior himself, indicating to him, if necessary, when he is performing well. Therefore, each approach can contribute uniquely to effective learning. All of these techniques are largely interpersonal and have traditionally been performed or facilitated by teachers, though some can be presented more efficiently by textbooks, teaching machines, films, or computer-assisted instruction.

CHAPTER FOUR

PERSUASION IN THE CLASSROOM

Is teaching a miniature form of mass communication and persuasion? Compare the teacher in the classroom with the announcer in a television commercial. The commercial aims at changing your beliefs and attitudes but, most important of all, it attempts to affect your behavior and decisions out in the "real world." Is schooling different in this respect? Obviously, the specific behavior, decisions, and attitudes being modified in the two situations are different. What is valued by the school differs from commercial values—we hope. However, this content difference might not require different social psychological principles. The advantage of noting the similarity of teaching to mass communication and persuasion lies in the availability of a large body of experimental research in the latter area which we may apply to teaching. The limitations of the comparison are important and should be considered by the reader, though that discussion will be postponed until later in the chapter.

The history of interest in the principles of mass persuasion goes back at least to the study of rhetoric in classical Greece. The concern there was to learn how to write, embellish, memorize, and present speeches which would effectively sway the public to the speaker's position. Much has been written on this topic, primarily prescriptive texts and essays. However, systematic and extensive experimental study has been carried out only in the past twenty-five years.

Much of the recent research was either initiated or stimulated by the work of Carl Hovland, Irving Janis, and Harold Kelley (1953), as published in their volume *Communication and Persuasion.* One of the problems they investigated derived from the old question of whether emotional appeals are more effective than rational appeals. They compared the effects of using low, moderate, and high levels of threat in attempts to persuade groups of children to change their toothbrushing habits. The highest threat level included a film demonstrating surgery on serious gum disorders. The lowest threat level merely mentioned the possibility of getting cavities. In this study and a few subsequent investigations (Janis and Feshbach, 1953), it was found that lower fear levels were more effective in inducing the desired change in behavior. However, later research has at least as frequently demonstrated that higher levels of fear are more effective. One recent review (McGuire, 1969) has indicated that for the greatest effectiveness the level of fear employed must be matched to the seriousness or significance of the issue. Another investigation (Haefner, 1965) found that higher levels of threat were more effective with lower-class children, while lower threat levels were more effective with middle-class children.

What implications do these findings have for the teaching situation? In teaching, emotional arousal of the pupils may occur in two contexts, in managing or motivating the students and in the content of the lessons. Clearly, there are many teachers who threaten pupils with lowered grades, being "left back," getting extra assignments, staying after school, going to the principal's office, or other punishments to force the pupils to accept their demands. Many other teachers who do not explicitly employ threats depend upon the child's fear of failure in school to motivate "appropriate" behavior. While much has been written on the subject, there is little objective evidence on the positive or negative consequences of the use of threats in maintaining discipline.

Kounin and his colleagues have carried out a series of "Explorations in Classroom Management" (1963), which examine the effects of varied techniques for handling student "misbehavior." In one study with groups of volunteer eighth and ninth graders in a new classroom setting, a student (cooperating with the experimenter) got up and sharpened a pencil during a presentation of slides by the teacher. The teacher then employed one of three "desist" techniques predesignated by the experimenter. She either rebuked the child intensely and physically put him back in his seat, simply reprimanded him, or ignored him. The severe reprimand led other children to rate the deviant behavior of the pupil as more serious, to indicate that there was greater interference with the ongoing event, that the teacher was overreacting, and that it upset them more. The mild reprimand led to reports of greatest teacher fairness and highest attention to the lesson. Ignoring the deviant behavior resulted in the other children's believing there would be a recurrence of the misbehavior. The studies in this series also suggest the distressing and distracting aspects of punitive teacher behavior.

When we move from teacher-management threats to content with strong emotional components, the situation gets more complex. In the study of fear appeals mentioned above, the fear was associated with dental disease, and therefore may be considered to be a veiled threat from the communicator that "if you don't do what you're supposed to, that's what will happen to you." As in the management situation, the fear is associated with not fulfilling the demands of the communicator. In the case of other topics, students may be emotionally aroused accidentally or intentionally by a teacher though no action is prescribed. Class discussions of democracy, communism, or nationalism may be structured by the teacher to arouse student emotional involvement to facilitate verbal interchange among the students. The result may be different from that anticipated. A student may identify the teacher as the object of the aroused hostility. If the issue is one on which the whole community has hostile feelings, the teacher's position may be endangered. In a recent situation a faculty member at a state college dramatically illustrated the significance of symbols by burning a miniature American flag. He was removed from his teaching position. A high school teacher in a nearby community, hoping to use active student discussion of controversies as a method of getting students to think, raised in discussion the issue of the legitimacy of the college teacher's removal. Following the heated discussion in class, one student wrote a letter to the local newspaper stating that his teacher was advocating flag-burning. Various "patriotic" persons and organizations responded by placing pressure on the school board, which then dismissed the teacher without a review of her case.

COMMITMENT

It is apparent that emotional involvement of students may stimulate learning but that it may also result in destructive conflict between student and teacher. Emotional arousal may have a detrimental effect if the student's commitment to his position is very strong, and is based on such intense personal needs and/or social support that the position cannot readily be modified. A threat to the position is then reacted to as an attack on the self, and the person frequently becomes even more entrenched in his initial position. This is known as the "boomerang effect" in the mass communications literature.

This effect of personal commitment upon attitude change has been extensively studied within the framework of Festinger's "Theory of Cognitive Dissonance" (1957). This theory holds that whenever a person has two inconsistent beliefs or thoughts, there will be some change in the pattern of beliefs to resolve this dissonance. Cognitive dissonance is defined as the simultaneous belief in two or more incompatible ideas. The theory focuses on the situation in which an existing belief, e.g., "I am honest," is challenged by a new observation, e.g., "I have just cheated on a test." The theory states that there will be some change in beliefs to reduce this incompatibility, e.g., "That was not really cheating" or "I am basically honest but also practical" or "Cheating is the only just response to an unfair test."

The earlier illustration of the fired schoolteacher can be analyzed here using the principles of dissonance theory. Before Mrs. Jones brought up the flag-burning issue, the children and the community probably believed: (1) "A teacher is someone who knows what is right and wrong"; (2) "Burning the flag is terribly wrong and should be punished"; and (3) "Mrs. Jones is a teacher." The children's observations in class suggested a fourth belief, incompatible with the others: "Mrs. Jones said that someone who burns the flag might be right and should not be punished." This is an instance of cognitive dissonance. One resolution of the dissonance was presented by the school board. They demanded that Mrs. Jones no longer be a teacher because she did not know right from wrong. If we substitute "Mrs. Jones is not acceptable as a teacher" for "Mrs. Jones is a teacher," the dissonance is removed. Other resolutions were possible, of course. The dissonance might have been reduced by the students' changing their attitude about flag-burning. If we substituted for the second belief, "Burning the flag is not *always* wrong" we no longer find the set of beliefs incompatible. This apparently was an inconceivable substitution of beliefs for some of Mrs. Jones' students, or for the superpatriotic organizations which applied pressure on the school board to fire Mrs. Jones.

Dissonance theory has been fruitful in suggesting one potentially useful approach to changing beliefs. The technique is to get the learner *voluntarily* to commit himself publicly to a new position.

An early study by Festinger and Carlsmith (1959) serves to illustrate how this phenomenon has been explored. College students were asked to participate in an experiment which turned out to be very boring. They were then asked to cooperate with the experimenter in recruiting other college students to be subjects by telling these persons how interesting the study was. The recruiters were paid either one dollar or twenty dollars for the recruitment talk; then they were asked to rate their own liking for the initial boring experiment. The authors of the study predicted—and found—that those who were paid the lesser amount (one dollar) would report more favorable attitudes than those who were paid much more (twenty dollars). This prediction and finding was dramatic because both common sense and learning theory would suggest that the greater the reward, the more likely subjects would be to report liking the boring task. How does cognitive dissonance theory predict the opposite?

First of all, the beliefs involved must be examined. All subjects initially *disliked the boring task.* All subjects experienced dissonance in that they publicly *committed themselves when they told others that they thought it was an interesting task.* Given this dissonance, how could it be resolved? Those who were paid twenty dollars could reduce dissonance by recognizing that the amount of money offered made it legitimate to tell a lie. (After all, it was only an experiment and twenty dollars is a lot of money for a few minutes' work.) Those who were paid only a dollar could not justify their lying on the basis of a good bribe. One dollar, it seems, is just not enough. Therefore, they had to reduce the dissonance between their beliefs (task was boring) and their public statement (task was fun) by changing their beliefs.

An application of the effects of public commitment to the classroom is the employment of "role playing" techniques. A student is asked to play a role which emphasizes a position he disagrees with. If the teacher does not apply too much pressure, the student's attempt to defend a position contrary to his own may lead him to reconsider his own beliefs. The act of publicly presenting a set of beliefs necessitates that one think about the positive features of the argument as well as identifying himself with it. A number of studies have shown that role playing can lead to attitude change (Cohen, 1964). Moreover, if there is some support for the new attitudes either by those around the individual or from new information he obtains, these changes may become lasting.

Role playing may also be used to cope with interpersonal problems in the classroom or with academic learning. A student who constantly interrupts the teacher or others may be asked to teach the class so that he may see what the effects of such interruptions are. A boy who continually leads the girl sitting next to him to cry may be asked to exchange roles with her so that he can see the implications of his behavior. An American student may be asked to play the role of the Russian Ambassador to the United Nations.

IMMUNIZATION AGAINST ATTITUDE CHANGE

One of the characteristics of role playing which produces a potential for changing attitudes is that the individual in his presentation must consider arguments and justifications for positions to which he would otherwise not be exposed. This experience can also be used to "immunize" an individual against attempts to change his attitudes. McGuire (1964) and his colleagues raised the question of the applicability of the medical immunization analogy to making individuals resistant to external influence attempts. In other words, would a mild dose of opposing arguments prepare the person to ward off strong opposing arguments? In a series of research studies, McGuire and his colleagues demonstrated that if individuals are asked to defend themselves against a moderate counterargument to their beliefs, they tend to become resistant to extremely strong influence attempts at a later time. This was shown to be true whether the stronger influence attempts were of the same type as the moderate one or quite different. They also showed that an individual who had to defend himself against moderate counterarguments had more resistance to later much stronger influence attempts than those who had made arguments in support of their beliefs. Generally, the reason for the individual's increased resistance or his "immunization" were twofold; first, he felt that the arguments of the persuasive attempts were not credible; and second, the immunized individual thought up more arguments and arguments of better quality in support of his original beliefs than did the nonimmunized individual.

All the McGuire experiments were based on beliefs related to cultural truisms; that is, beliefs that are so widely shared by the individual and others with whom he comes in contact that he would not have heard them attacked and would probably doubt that such an attack were possible. Some examples of such cultural truisms are: "It's a good idea to brush your teeth after every meal if at all possible"; and "Mental illness is not contagious." While the use of such cultural truisms may limit the applicability of the inoculation and immunization demonstrated in these experiments, the experiments raise certain issues for teachers. Generally, when teachers present the basic tenets of democracy—the equality of men, the basic rights of all individuals—the students are expected to dutifully accept them. But, as these experiments have shown, the technique of supportive arguments is much less effective than having to defend one's cultural truisms against moderately contradictory counterarguments. Therefore, teachers who are trying to create strong beliefs about core cultural values and make them resistant to change should place their students in situations with moderate arguments opposing these core beliefs. Instead of learning to say that the United States of America is great, the student needs to be able to answer moderate arguments claiming that the U.S. is weak, immoral, and dangerous.

THE PERSUADER

The previous discussion dealt with the importance of exposure to both viewpoints in the situation where one is trying to defend himself against another's arguments. Suppose you are in the position of the persuader: Should you present only one side of the argument, avoiding any topic which might raise questions about the adequacy of your position? The advertiser is unlikely to point out that his product is smaller or costlier than others. But we have all used and heard arguments ("soft-sell") where the persuader throws in well-known limitations of his product and then proceeds to his main argument. Avis Rent-A-Car always reminds us it is not the largest car rental agency. Volkswagen commercials are known for the humorous way they treat the unpopular size and shape of their products; the boxlike qualities of their minibus are illustrated by constructing a model bus out of a shoebox, the small sedan is illustrated by the double bass sticking up through the sunroof, etc. Of course, in all these cases, the advertisement then goes on to emphasize positive features of the product.

There is evidence that such two-sided arguments are valuable when the audience is skeptical about the message and knowledgeable about the counterarguments. On the other hand, the two-sided argument is less successful where the weaknesses of the main argument are unknown, where the audience has great respect for the authority presenting the argument, and where the audience is ready to accept the message.

The decision on whether to employ one-sided or two-sided arguments in teaching must consider the following: (1) the fact that we place great value on rational and personal choice in our society, which implies the one-sided argument is opposed to our values; and (2) the fact that one of the purposes of teaching is to provide accurate rather than biased information. On the other hand, a two-sided argument by a teacher may fail to clarify what the valued position is in our society or may mislead the students into believing that the teacher holds the opposite value. Particularly problematic, as in the flag-burning lessons, is the case where the community is unready to hear the opposite side and a presentation of the unaccepted argument results in rejection of the teacher, that is, in the complete rejection of the teacher's credibility.

The effect of communicator credibility upon persuasive influence has been extensively studied and, as one might suspect, it has often been found that the more credible the communicator, the greater his ability to change beliefs. However, other studies show that this effect of credibility upon our attitudes does not persist (Hovland and Weiss, 1965; Kelman and Hovland, 1953). One interpretation of this finding is that just after listening to a highly respected speaker, we may be greatly influenced by his statements, but as we forget who stated the beliefs, we are likely to give them less credence and therefore to return to our original beliefs. Similarly, immediately after listening to a disliked speaker, we may be completely unswayed or even strengthened in our original position, but as we forget the source of the arguments, they begin to affect our beliefs and change them as much as do the statements of the more credible speaker.

In the classroom, the teacher may be upset by the student who refuses to accept anything, who seems to have no respect for "authority." The teacher may feel that the student is learning nothing about history because he always doubts the teacher's interpretations. However, such a student may in the long run demonstrate considerable understanding of the teacher's point of view and, in fact, may come to accept it as his own, once he no longer is fighting the idea as the teacher's idea but simply remembers its content. This same principle, however, seems to argue against free discussion in the classroom, since students may remember their classmates' erroneous interpretations as well as their teacher's more "appropriate" statements. While at the time they could have easily told you which was the right answer, in the future all the answers may be considered relatively equal in weight. This suggests that the teacher get in the "final word" on each discussion, treating and evaluating the erroneous arguments so that the student may recall the logic by which the argument can be countered. This makes the questionable assumption that the later logic will be as well remembered as the earlier argument.

We have been discussing the effect of teacher credibility. The question arises as to whether, indeed, the teacher has a high credibility. Typically he does, if for no other reason than that the age and education gap between teacher and student generally is sufficient to establish the teacher's authority as a valid communicator. But one can certainly think of exceptions—the uninspired, mediocre teacher with a group of honor students, the lower-class Negro child who distrusts the white middle-class teacher, or the teacher trying to play expert in the realm of values.

Parallel to the credibility of the teacher is the credulity of the pupil. There is some evidence that persuasibility is higher among those with lower self-esteem (Janis, 1954). If failure in school leads to lowered self-esteem, then students who have failed should be most malleable. This seems to contradict common experience in the classroom. Perhaps this is because the student may attribute his failure to the teacher and thus hostility to the teacher accompanies reduced self-esteem. Under such conditions, defensive behavior and the avoidance of exposure to further learning experiences may result. Furthermore, the typical failure in school is not followed by the teacher's insight into what steps in acquiring information or skills are feasible for the student at that point in time. Thus, even if motivated to respond by accepting the teacher's instructions, the pupil may not be competent to do so. It is easy to observe numerous instances in teaching where the inadequate student tries harder to conform to the teacher's demands than the more adequate student, but can do so only in a superficial or grossly inaccurate manner.

SITUATIONAL FACTORS

In addition to persuader and audience (e.g., student) characteristics which facilitate or impede attitude change, situational characteristics are also crucial. An interesting comparison has been made between the high degree of influence of persuaders in laboratory studies and the ineffectiveness of natural mass communication influence attempts as presented through the mass media (Hovland, 1959). Study after study has shown that attempts to change public opinion through the mass media have met with failure—much to the chagrin of governments and large organizations (McGuire, 1969). Some of the reasons for the difference between the success in the laboratory and the failure in the natural setting may be as follows: the mass communicator must face the possibility of not reaching his audience because he is literally "turned off" or never "turned on" or because competing positions are heard by the listener, or because the motivation of the mass communicator is so blatantly manipulative and oriented to needs other than those of the audience. Furthermore, the real issues presented in the mass media are often ones on which the listener has his own strong opinions and he usually has support for these beliefs among his friends and acquaintances. By contrast, in the experimental situation the listener can only figuratively turn the persuader off (he has to hear the message), and the presentation of alternative views (if any) is under the control of the experimenter. Furthermore, the status of the communicator is generally established, the issue is usually one on which the listener has no strong beliefs and, finally, there is usually no opportunity for the listener to consult with friends or acquaintances, or even others in the experimental situation.

If one tries to place the classroom teaching situation in terms of its resemblance to the natural mass communications situation or the laboratory situation, one is struck with how similar the classroom is to the laboratory. The college student has relatively little choice about what beliefs he will be exposed to in the classroom, and the younger student has almost no choice at all. (It is no wonder that a variety of "shutting out" techniques are employed by students, and that maintaining attention is one of the greatest problems of the instructor.) Furthermore, as in the laboratory, credibility of the communicator (the teacher) is high, students often have no strongly conflicting beliefs on the content being taught, and there is little classroom consulting with peers about the content being presented. Finally, the teacher has control over pupil rewards and punishments. The teacher, like the experimenter, has a tremendous advantage over the mass media.

This advantage of classroom teaching is bought at a high price, namely, coercion. What are some of the alternatives to maintaining such tight control over the teaching situation? Classroom groups can be allowed to operate in a way similar to the natural operation of friendship groups in screening mass communications. The group members can make certain decisions about what they should have to listen to or study and when, and can decide whether the teacher or lesson has made its case convincingly. This intrusion of the group between the teacher and pupil may reduce efficiency, but the resulting changes in beliefs could be more strongly held. One of the main reasons for this is the greater involvement of students in the learning process. However, in most cases the group could not or would not effectively refute the teacher's presentations, since its members are generally not acceptable as a credible source for academic learning. They could, however, offer alternative solutions.

PERSUADER STYLE

The particular interpersonal techniques used in teaching and persuasion may have a great influence on the patterns of thought as well as the content of beliefs of the listener or learner. It may be that for some of us thought is like inner lecturing, for others like an inner debate, and for still others, thought may be in question-answer form. In other words, all the devices which are used in teaching and persuading may have their parallel in our thinking. This implies two things: first, the style of thinking derives from exposure to particular styles of communication, persuasion, and teaching; second, the listener may learn better when the style of thinking that he brings to the learning situation matches the presentation style of the teacher. There is some evidence that the middle-class mother talks to her children differently than the lower-class mother does; the middle-class mother tends to give reasons for what she says, whereas the lower-class mother tends to demand that children listen to her because she's the mother. This would seem to prepare the middle-class child for the kind of thought required for *optimum* learning in school. Furthermore, this preparation enables the teacher to reduce the degree of coercion in the middle-class school. In contrast, the lower-class child has less adequate techniques for thought and poor preparation to follow the kind of teaching which should go on in school (Strodtbeck, 1965). Instead, he is more prepared for coercion and gets it in the lower-class school. The teachers seem to perceive that this is the only style to which these children can respond.

Similar to the influence of persuader or teacher style upon style of thought is the impact of the mass media upon mode of thought. McLuhan (1964) has suggested that the invention of printing had a tremendous impact on the style of thought processes, and that the current exposure to the electronic media, radio and television, has again greatly influenced patterns of thinking. Each medium requires a different kind of audience participation and this influences the way people react to everything else; for example, today's television watchers read differently than pre-TV readers. From McLuhan's point of view, the impact of TV on the educational process lies not in the changes in time spent reading nor in the use of TV in teaching, but rather in the influence of growing up as a TV watcher on the way one listens to a lecture, participates in a discussion, or reads a book.

CONCLUSION

Although our values about education lead us to reject the parallel of teaching and selling, there is much to be learned from examining teaching as persuasive communication. However, our values must enter the decision as to what persuasive methods are acceptable. Efficiency of communication is certainly not our only value. Methods which leave the listener freedom of choice are most consistent with the ideals of a democracy. Furthermore, those persuasive methods which themselves include rational presentation of alternatives seem most likely to lead to internalized dialogue as a mode of thought. This style of thinking may, in turn, lead to a readiness to listen to alternative points of view. It is therefore essential to take into account the cognitive consequences of the modes of communication employed in teaching and the mass media.

CHAPTER FIVE

LEADERSHIP IN THE CLASSROOM

Is a teacher a leader in the classroom? Such a question seems to be easily answered: of course! Yet, a leader can be defined in a number of ways that make this answer less obvious. A leader can be someone who is selected by the group to represent it; as such, the teacher is not a leader and it is unlikely that students, if they had a choice, would select him.

Another definition of a leader is that he epitomizes the values and traits of group members. But teachers and students would agree that this definition does not fit. Teachers would maintain that one of their functions is to change their students, hence to epitomize student values and traits that should be changed would be unacceptable to them. Students would probably state that the teacher doesn't really understand them.

A third possible definition of a leader is that he is the person whose actions are primarily directed at obtaining maximum satisfaction for group members. Again, both teachers and students would maintain that this is not the role of a teacher; rather, a teacher is to educate and train students in a manner which may lead to immediate dissatisfaction and discomfort for them.

If teachers do not fulfill any of the above definitions of a leader, how can we refer to them as leaders in the classroom? We do know, of course, that teachers exert considerable influence in the classroom, but this influence is not derived from the wishes of the students; rather, it emerges from the concept of school as an institution which formally designates the teacher as the most powerful individual in the classroom. To the extent that students exert influence in a classroom, and they surely do, they may do so as a result of their being elected, or epitomizing student values and traits, or maximizing satisfaction for group members.

In this chapter, we shall discuss a number of concepts that relate to leadership in the classroom. We shall discuss informal and formal leadership and the sources from which teachers and other leaders derive their power, as well as the relationship between leadership styles and group processes. In the latter discussion we will analyze from a methodological point of view the classical study of democratic, autocratic, and laissez-faire leadership.

TEACHER POWER VERSUS STUDENT POWER

There is surely no question about who is formally designated as leader in the classroom. Nor is there any doubt that the teacher typically is the only one given the responsibility and specific powers by the school system to wield considerable influence over students in the classroom. Yet informal sources of influence available to students may, in certain circumstances, be as great as the formal sources supporting the teacher's role. In our earlier illustration of a "showdown" between a rebellious student and an aggressive teacher, the teacher's formal sources of authority were not enough. He felt he needed to use physical strength to limit the leadership challenge of the student. He was interpreting the student's refusal to obey a simple request and the student's curse as meaning "I dare you to make me do it. I don't think you can match me in a physical battle and that's all that counts here in determining who is boss."

The usurping of power by students through physical strength or threat is obviously not the only manner in which students may gain influence in the classroom. In some settings, students are intentionally given responsibility for influencing policy. Consider an extreme case, Summerhill, the experimental private residential school in England where attendance at classes is voluntary, where grades are not given, and where the student body and faculty meet together to determine policy, each student and faculty member having an equal vote (Neill, 1960). What powers remain for the teacher? The ability of the teacher to influence students in a place like Summerhill depends on his ability to provide desired information, teach desired skills, or maintain interest. He may still have much more than an equal share of power with students because of his age, education, intelligence, and skills, but by comparison with the traditional classroom teacher the gap in degree of influence between teacher and pupil is certainly narrowed and the actions the teacher must take to influence his students are quite different. He cannot expect them to obey him simply because he is the teacher. Nor can he depend on their being there to hear him unless he can make them feel he is contributing something they desire.

In a way, the distribution of power between faculty and pupils at Summerhill resembles a predominantly lower-class "inner city" school much more than it resembles the relative power of teacher and students in the middle-class school. Though middle-class schools are more likely to be enlightened, to delegate certain responsibilities to students, and to have teachers who use student-centered teaching methods, the power is given to students somewhat in the manner of a benevolent dictatorship. Students may participate to the extent that they mirror the values of the school and its teachers. The student accepts the legitimacy of the teacher as a leader because of a resemblance to the student's own parents and because he has been taught to value the rewards dispensed in school. The teacher is seen as a legitimate leader regardless of competency to teach.

For the Negro students in the ghetto school, the situation is quite different. The student, because of class, language, and racial differences, cannot readily substitute the teacher for his parents, and does not bring to school a set of behaviors and values which the school will reward. As a result, the teacher cannot assume he is a legitimate leader but, as in Summerhill, he has to earn his legitimacy through competence in meeting the student's needs and desires. There are certain other resemblances to Summerhill. Attendance may be required at all public schools but pupil norms in the ghetto school may strongly support truancy. Thus, as in Summerhill, the teacher may even have to earn his right to have the pupils attend his class. Though the students at Summerhill are from the middle class, they resemble those in ghetto schools in that many of them had not been responsive to the demands of the traditional school. The "disadvantaged" pupil is still in that kind of school and suffering. Summerhill explicitly provides students with the power that the ghetto child must usurp.

To summarize, the teacher is given certain responsibilities by the school and a certain amount of authority. In the eyes of the school, he is a legitimate object of respect—that is, he is deserving of respect—and should be listened to. However, the ultimate source of his legitimacy in terms of his ability to communicate to and teach students is the students themselves. If they respect the teacher's authority and competence he has legitimacy in the classroom; if they do not, no amount of formal statements will provide him with it. He can grade and fail the students on the basis of the authority given him by the school; he can teach them only on the authority that the students grant him on the basis of his concern for them and his competence.

SOURCES OF POWER

Those individuals who have been formally designated as leaders by an organization, or appointed by one who has authority in an organization, or who have been formally elected in a recognized election, are often called formal leaders. Those leaders who emerge from a group as a result of their recognized abilities to accomplish tasks, to fill the social or emotional needs of others, or because of their attractiveness (often called "charisma") are usually called informal leaders.

The distinction between these two types of leaders is essential because of the different way in which they are able to influence their followers. Formal leaders usually have resources or power derived from their organizational position: a teacher can fail a student; a teacher-appointed student leader can tell the teacher that another student is "bad," thereby leading to that student's punishment by the teacher; and an elected student represents the wishes of students. On the other hand, informal leaders derive their ability to influence others from personal qualities which attract others. If the leader should fail to be attractive, i.e., if his personal qualities should fail to satisfy others, he may be deposed as a leader. In one case (formal), the leader fills a position from which he derives his ability to influence; in the other case (informal), the leader derives his ability to influence others from his personal resources.

Good leadership for a formal leader, however, depends upon his ability to become an informal leader at the same time. In order to analyze why this is so, it is helpful to examine the variety of sources of power open to leaders. Five such sources are the following: (1) reward power, or ability to give rewards for desired behavior; (2) coercive power, or ability to punish undesired behaviors; (3) referent power, or being looked up to as models for followers' behavior; (4) expert power, or ability to provide specialized desired knowledge; and (5) legitimate power, or being considered as legitimate leaders by the followers (French and Raven, 1960).

The teacher, quite obviously, has both reward and punishment (or coercion) at his command. He can give students good grades or fail them, or he can accept them or reject them. However, there is a problem with this kind of power, especially coercive power. The only time that it is effective is when the teacher is present in the same situation as the student. Since he administers directly the rewards or punishments he can only influence the student through his constant surveillance. Thus, if this is the only type of power he uses, the students may follow his wishes in his presence but disregard them when he leaves the room. Furthermore, the effective use of reward or punishment requires that students perceive that these outcomes will occur if they do or don't obey the leader. The teacher who uses pupil failure as a threat to keep the noisy class in order may find he is unsuccessful because his pupils know that he won't use such a severe punishment for a mild infraction. Finally, rewards and punishment are a limited source of power because they can be *used up*. If a teacher continually punishes students he may find that future punishment has little effect. In fact he may find a "boomerang effect"; whenever he threatens or punishes his students they do quite the reverse of what he desires. The student who has been to the principal's office several times knows he will survive and has developed ways of coping with the situation. He may enjoy upsetting the teacher more than he worries about what will happen to him. Similarly, the student who has failed three times no longer has anything to lose by being failed again. Too many rewards can also be used up. The teacher who tells all his pupils they are wonderful for everything they do finds that they soon ignore his praise.

Nevertheless, frequent use of reward may strengthen the teacher's leadership role. A teacher who frequently rewards a student may become a very attractive person to the student, which may lead him to want to be similar to the teacher. Thus the teacher develops a new type of influence over the students called "referent power" or power based on identification.

Because the student wants to be like the teacher and be close to him, he may follow the desires of the teacher, whether or not the latter is present or requests that the student do so. The important ingredient for the student is that his relationship to the teacher be maintained. As a result, the teacher gains a new base of power. This new source of power is typical of informal leaders, who are listened to not because their followers have to listen, but because they want to. Moreover, the leader need not request such behavior, and therefore cannot easily use up this resource. Thus the formal leader who has referent power may increase his resources without risking his formal basis of power, i.e., rewards and punishments.

Power gained through expert knowledge has similar advantages. The leader need not attempt directly to influence his followers. If the students feel that a teacher is very competent, or if patients feel their doctor is able, then they will listen to him because they want to learn or get well. However, the perceived expertise must be validated from time to time. The teacher may lose his expert power if the students find him often wrong. This power is limited to specific situations in which expertise is established.

Informal type of leadership achieves influence because the follower *wants* to be influenced, rather than vice versa. It is another component of what we previously referred to as good leadership. But why should we label this "good?" The answer is that the teacher—who is given certain rights and responsibilities by the school and who is perceived as a legitimate leader by the students—will have great difficulty in teaching and leading the students if he must always resort to punishments or rewards. The students will learn not because they want to but because of external forces which push them. If the teacher wants to avoid being the policeman he must in some way relate to the students so that they begin to enjoy learning. A *beginning* step in this attempt to influence the students is for the teacher to use himself as a frame of reference for them. If the teacher is liked and if the students respect him because of his concern for their growth, then they may begin to use him as a model for themselves. At first, this may be achieved by the proper use of reward power, but it must continue through the students' perception of the teacher's concern for them as well as the enjoyment of the learning and teaching process. A teacher's competence in the subject matter will reinforce this process. In short, the teacher who has gained referent and expert power has increased his power as a leader and thereby increased his ability to influence his students. Furthermore, this is even more important than merely increasing reward or coercive power because this new increase results from the desires of the students themselves.

INFORMAL LEADERSHIP

Previous mention has been made of the informal leadership that develops among students in a classroom. The question arises as to how this is achieved. Considerable research by Bales (1958) and his colleagues has been carried out in the last decade on the dynamics of leaderless groups—groups which begin without any assigned or elected leader—which were given group problem-solving tasks to perform. The research indicated that after working together for a short period of time, one or more persons with special problem-solving skills became identified and were looked to for direction in handling the task. Other individuals emerged who seemed to specialize in reducing tensions among group members and had particular influence in this "social-emotional" sphere.

These results can be related to the classroom setting in two ways. First the students themselves develop task leaders among themselves who are seen as the most competent problem solvers. Such a student may be the most intelligent student or the best athlete; for the most part, other students look to this task leader for guidance. Often, however, the task leader in a classroom as well as in the laboratory experiment tends to be somewhat abrasive, controlling, or directive. This results from his concern to get a job done and his attempt to get others to perform in a way that will achieve group goals.

Especially in formerly leaderless groups or in a classroom, other students do not take too kindly to being pushed or directed. Such leader behavior can result in a considerable degree of tension. In order to avoid this potentially disruptive force, another student, who is usually very well liked by the group, attempts to reduce the tension by cracking jokes, smiling, teasing, or any one of a number of other tricks. This separation of functions enables both types of leaders to effectively move the group towards its goal.

It should be noted that there are many situations in which these two types of functions are performed by the same person. These people have been labeled by researchers as "great men." It is probable that in leaderless or classroom groups the two functions will tend to be separate due to the antagonism created by the leader in pushing the group towards its goal.

The second application to the classroom setting is seen in the relationship between teacher and student. In general, teachers maintain their greatest control in the task area, i.e., in facilitating academic achievement. This concentration may leave a gap in the socio-emotional or tension reduction area in which students can be most effective. Thus the teacher may be seen as a task leader and the most popular student may be seen as the socio-emotional leader.

The question can be raised, How can a leadership position which emerges from a leaderless group be maintained? How does the classroom leader remain in his position? Hollander (1958) has attempted to answer this question by reference to experimental and "real life" situations. In a number of laboratory settings he found that individuals who are more competent in performing a task at the beginning of the experiment seem to accumulate a "credit" in the eyes of their fellow group members. Similarly, in group situations one often finds that those who emerge as leaders usually have, for a time, very carefully conformed to norms of the group and have usually performed better than other group members. This seems to be true for group as well as student leaders. One often finds that gang leaders fight less than newcomers to the group who have to prove themselves. The leaders have previously demonstrated their superior competence and only rarely have to prove it again; newcomers and others have not built up this "credit" and must continually perform in order to be accepted.

Hollander calls these credits "idiosyncrasy credits" because they enable the leader to behave, at times, independently of group norms. This has important implications for creative leadership. If a leader is to be effective in helping his group he must continually develop innovations for making the group more effective. Innovation requires risk and the potential for failure. If the leader did not have the accumulated idiosyncrasy credits such innovation might be too risky for his own position and he probably would not attempt it. This also applies to a good teacher. Such a teacher is expected to be innovative and often is because he is not afraid of losing his reputation. He has credits which he can use up before his reputation changes. The mediocre teacher is usually afraid to innovate because of his fear of failure and the reduction in his already limited reputation. He has few credits and failure potentially means a lower evaluation of him by others.

LEADERSHIP STYLE OF THE TEACHER

It is difficult for anyone who has been a student of many teachers not to recognize tremendous differences in the manner in which the teacher fulfills his role. After subject competence, the characteristic which strikes us most is the extent to which the teacher is directive, structured, and controlling on the one hand or nondirective, unstructured, and permissive on the other.

Two of the best-known sources of influence on the topic of directive teaching are the writings of Carl Rogers (1951) on the nondirective approach to counseling and reports of the research of Lewin and his followers Lippitt and White (1965) on autocratic versus democratic leadership. Both Rogers and Lewin draw upon their values at least as much as upon objective evidence. Rogers' nondirective approach is based on a respect for the other person and Lewin's on a valuation of the group member and democratic process. To the extent that Rogers believes it is not *right* to attempt to manipulate or control his client, but only to be sensitive and responsive to his needs, the nondirective approach is a dogma or creed and not a scientifically testable hypothesis about what works. Similarly, to the extent that Lewin's followers believe that autocratic leadership is *wrong* because it is violating the basic need of the group to participate, there is no way of demonstrating the belief to be correct. So, if you believe that the only way to teach your students is to be permissive, it would be difficult for any evidence to refute your belief. However, these men and their followers are "behavioral scientists" and have been greatly concerned with scientific demonstration of the *effectiveness* of the interpersonal relationships they are proposing. Since the Lippitt and White (1965) study of autocratic versus democratic leadership is perhaps the best known among educators, it will be discussed in some detail here.

Kurt Lewin and his students were excited about the possibility of simulating and studying naturally occurring group processes in a controlled experimental situation. In the first of two studies of leadership phenomena carried out around 1940, Ronald Lippitt acted as leader for two similar "hobby" groups, each with five eleven-year-old children, which met over a period of several weeks. For one of the groups he played the role of "autocratic" leader, leaving no decisions to group members and fully controlling the direction of all activities. For the second group, Lippitt "democratically" made no decisions himself but encouraged group members to organize, plan, and make decisions regarding their activities. In both groups, the leader tried to be friendly. This is important since autocratic leadership is often thought of as punitive. The experimenter did not, however, wish to "load the dice" in favor of democratic leadership. Careful observation and recording was carried out during all group sessions. In this first study it was found that the autocratic group behaved in a much more aggressive, destructive fashion than the democratic group.

This first investigation demonstrated the feasibility of setting up and studying groups in a controlled setting and experimentally influencing their patterns of interaction. Furthermore, the results suggested some important influences of leadership style upon the interaction and performance of group members. However, the study was limited in its scientific controls.

Consider trying to make *general* statements about autocratic and democratic leadership based on observations of only one leader playing the two roles, especially when this leader was the experimenter, who could hardly be considered neutral with regard to desired experimental outcomes. Consider further the problem of trying to come to conclusions about the difference between the two types of leadership when each leadership style was tried with a different group, and each with only one group. The aggressiveness found under autocratic leadership might have resulted from the presence of one particularly hostile boy in the autocratic group. To overcome the limitations of Lippitt's study, a second investigation was carried out.

In the second study, four groups of children and four leaders were employed. The groups met for three six-week sessions, each time with a different leader. Each leader met with three of the groups during the experiment. Furthermore, each leader and each group were scheduled to have the autocratic role once, the democratic role once, and one of these two leader roles again during the final session. This experimental design has much appeal when compared with the first study. Since the same group experiences both types of leadership at least once, we can compare the effects of democratic and autocratic leadership on the same group of children. Since there are four such groups, we can determine whether the phenomenon is peculiar to one group or occurs more generally. Since we have four different leaders, overall effects of leadership style cannot be attributed to the competence of a particular person in playing the role.

Examining the problems in carrying out this study and the nature of its findings should tell us much about leadership. The first major problem for the investigators came quite early, in the first three weeks of the first six-week session. One of the "democratic" leaders was having a terrible time getting his group (the "Charlie Chan" group) organized toward group goals and was apparently faced with a chaotic situation. The experimenters noted that this did not resemble the conditions of the original study, and that while the leader here was, as desired, maintaining little control over group goals and means, he was not adequately stimulating group procedures. This initially distressing incident led the experimenters to systematically examine this additional leadership style, which they came to call "laissez-faire" leadership. The leader of the Charlie Chan group was instructed not to make any further attempts at stimulating group decision-making and one other leader was asked to play the "laissez-faire" role during the second six-week session. Furthermore, all "democratic" leaders were instructed to give stronger emphasis to active organization of the group for decision-making.

This shift in the experimental design has serious implications for the logical stringency of the experiment. On the other hand, it represents a good illustration of the scientist's responsiveness to unexpected information gained in the course of investigation. It would be of value to think through the implications of the two alternative strategies in this case: (1) continuing with the original design as if nothing unusual had occurred; (2) altering the design when one's expectations as scientists have not been fulfilled.

If the experimenters had continued with their original plans, their findings would have been that attempts at democratic leadership, i.e., attempts to get group members to make their own decisions, may lead to a lack of organization and a disruptive climate with some groups and leaders. The experimenters would have to explain after the fact why the reactions differed more for some groups and leaders than for others. One of the explanations would be that some leaders made greater attempts at organizing the group for decision-making than others.

Altering the design allowed the investigators to systematically test one interpretation of the unexpected early findings. Instead of one instance of disruption in "democracy" they could observe additional occurrences, assuming that their explanation about the need for active organizing efforts was correct. One criticism of the study, then, is a critique of the way the study has been described and reported, not how it was carried out.

The investigators and later writers should have spoken about two kinds of "democracy" if they wished to use the term at all, and the study should have been described as two small experiments, not a single one in which the effects of three types of leadership had been tested.

What were the findings of the study? Did autocratic leadership result in the same aggressive reaction as in the first experiment? Only one group, the Charlie Chan group, showed an aggressive response to autocratic leadership. The other three groups were more submissive, showing less aggression than under democratic leadership.

Was the laissez-faire condition different from the democratic condition? Laissez-faire leadership groups did less work and poorer quality work than the democratically led groups. The democratic leaders were preferred, and more discontent was expressed toward laissez-faire leaders. These differences seemed largely a result of the lack of organization in the laissez-faire conditions.

Which was more efficient, democratic or autocratic leadership? Looking only at the amount of time spent absorbed in work, the autocratic groups out-performed the democratic groups. However, the democratic groups talked more about work and worked more when the leader left the room than did the autocratic groups. Which was better liked, autocratic or democratic leadership? The clear preference was for the democratic leader over the autocratic leader. Although some later studies have resulted in similar findings, there is considerable evidence to support the notion that the relative effectiveness of autocratic leadership and democratic leadership is dependent upon the characteristics of the task, the relationships among group members, and the power available to the leader.

An alternative to examining differences among leadership roles is to examine differences among groups of children. We shall continue to use the same investigation because of the thoroughness with which it has been reported (White and Lippitt, 1960), although, of course, the initial purpose of the investigation was not to explore the characteristics of the group members. However, the findings force recognition of the crucial importance of the peculiar characteristics of any group and its members. The Charlie Chan Club has already been mentioned on two occasions: once, as the group which forced the experimenters to explore the difference between democratic and laissez-faire leadership, and again as the only group in the second experiment which responded aggressively to autocratic leadership. Think how different the description of the results of this classical study would be without the Charlie Chan Club. What made the club so different?

Let's look at the members of this group. Reilly, the most popular boy in his grade, was an active, assertive leader who refused to recognize adult leadership. Fred, another member of the group, was described as sullenly defiant of adult leadership. Thus the personalities of these two group members and Reilly's considerable influence over group members may have been the reasons for the dramatic results from their group. Because of the popularity of this study and its tremendous influence on social scientists and educators these two boys probably have had as much impact on social psychological and educational theory and research as any subjects (or experimenters) in psychological investigation. Without them, the term "laissez-faire leadership" might not have developed and the conception of aggressive response to autocratic leadership might have been rejected as a "fluke" of the first study. We might speak of Reilly as a "leader" in social psychological research, having so unduly influenced the behavior and thinking of so many social psychologists and educators.

Reilly and the Charlie Chan Club provide us with many valuable insights having little to do with the original goals and design of the investigation. It is clear that knowledge of the intentions, role demands, and role behavior of an assigned leader are not sufficient to predict either performance or emotional outcomes of a group. The characteristics of members and their relationships to one another can drastically influence the patterns of group reaction to a leader attempting to play the same role in two or more different groups. It is also evident that formal assignment to a leadership position is not sufficient to focus sole leadership in that individual. The group must accept the leader. If it is unwilling to, or wishes to support other leaders, an informal pattern of control will be established at variance with the formally designated pattern. In this case, Reilly refused to give up his natural leadership position to the formally assigned adults and the group responded more positively to his leadership than to the adults' leadership attempts. Thus, while the adult leaders had legitimate power and to a limited extent reward and coercive power, Reilly had very strong referent power. In a situation where the group is short-lived and not part of a larger organizational authority structure, referent power (also called charismatic leadership) may be a more potent force.

This refusal to accept designated adult leadership is particularly crucial in the classroom, where the teacher is the formally designated leader. Leadership in the classroom clearly is not limited to teacher leadership but also includes student leadership. The first illustration in this book, in which an aggressive teacher and a rebellious student "locked horns," may be a good example of a teacher and a student competing for leadership positions. The teacher seems to realize that if he doesn't assert his control at this point, the whole pattern of classroom leadership will be shifted to the student—who, moreover, does not value the academic goals of the school. The teacher seems to view the alternatives as control or disorganization, autocratic or laissez-faire leadership. In an attempt to counteract the influence of the student he uses his coercive power over this particular student and attempts to invoke his legitimate power. If he is successful he will not have to use similar coercion over the other students. If he fails with this student his legitimacy in the eyes of the other students becomes quite weak and he must continually resort to coercion. As is often seen in the classroom, such use of force is inadequate. Even if the students do respond, their motivation is derived from external sources. Once the force is inadequate they will act to counteract its effect. The effective teacher knows that the best type of power in the classroom is that which results from his legitimacy, expertise, and attraction for the students (referent power).

This seems to be what Lewin and his associates were referring to. A group leader having an autocratic style tends to be very directive, very control-oriented, and, if necessary, punishment-oriented. Rather than using himself as an attractive force in the group he uses his *rights* as the appointed leader and forces the students to follow his will. The logical extension of the autocratic style would be that if the group members do not initially wish to follow his directions he will use reward and coercive power to ensure that they do.

On the other hand, the "democratic" leader, by permitting the group members to act on their own but with his encouragement (and therefore influence), is not invoking his *rights* as an appointed leader (although he still has them) but rather his expertise as a consultant and his attraction as a "good guy" who is concerned with the development of his group members (referent power). By successfully doing so, he is able to lead the group members to set their goals and carry out desired task functions without invoking rewards or punishments. The group members usually respond favorably to such a situation because they are doing things over which they themselves have some influence and also because they are following the wishes of a leader whom they like (referent) and respect (expert).

The concept of democratic leadership offers very interesting problems for the research-oriented social scientist. When we refer to the word democratic we are probably invoking the most value-laden term in our society. Imagine the consequences of saying that something "democratic" does not work. The second difficulty, uncorrelated with the first, is that the term "democratic" conveys too many different meanings. Try listing the things you mean by "democratic." Although "democratic leadership" was defined in the two experiments as a combination of "low control by leader" and "high stimulation of group procedures," and "autocratic leadership" as "high control by leader" and "low stimulation of group procedures" (White and Lippitt, 1960, p. 9), these definitions have not been clearly held by other writers. It is common, for example, to identify autocratic leadership with punitive leadership, although in the above experiments leaders tried to be friendly in all conditions. Frequently, the distinction between autocratic and democratic leadership is made solely on the basis of quantity of leader control, without regard to whether the leader stimulates or organizes the group to perform independently of him. This dichotomy is better referred to as directive-nondirective leadership. Although there are many reported studies and articles on the relative values of directive and nondirective teaching, and of teacher-centered and student-centered teaching, the research methods used are weak and their results are conflicting. A major problem of research in this area is the difficulty of deciding how to evaluate effectiveness of teaching procedures. The teacher-directed classroom may show better performance on a content-oriented achievement test whereas the student-centered classroom may be expected to perform better on a creative problem solving test (Anderson, 1963; McKeachie, 1963).[1]

One of the attractions of the Lewin, Lippitt, and White studies was their major departure from the earlier literature on leadership. Prior to the 1940's many psychologists were concerned with the particular kind of traits that leaders possess. What they often found was that there were no clear trends in leadership traits and that different studies often yielded contradictory results. These findings probably were affected by differences in group settings, role demands, and group members. Thus the Lewin studies indicated that leadership was to be sought more in the nature of the group atmosphere or roles performed by leaders than in the personalities of the leaders.

A second major breakthrough of these studies was the emphasis on observational techniques as a research tool. The most common research use of observational techniques has been in

---

1   See also discussion in Chapter 3.

studies of classrooms. Of the recent research emphasizing both the group setting (autocratic-democratic typology) and observational methods in the classroom, the work of Flanders is probably the best known and most extensive.

Flanders has developed a method of observing and recording teacher-pupil interaction which is termed "interaction analysis." The teacher's verbal behavior is classified into direct and indirect influence attempts. Direct attempts are subcategorized into "expresses or lectures about ideas or knowledge," "criticizes or degrades pupil behavior with intent to change it," and "justifies his own position or authority." Indirect influence attempts include "accepts, clarifies, and supports the ideas and feelings of pupils," "praises or encourages," "asks questions to stimulate pupils' participation in decision-making," and "asks questions to orient pupils to schoolwork or to the topic of discussion." This distinction between direct and indirect teacher influence clearly parallels the autocratic-democratic distinction. Under direct influence attempts by teachers, pupils are reported to participate less, to use direct influence techniques themselves, and to show more dislike for the class and the teacher than under indirect influence teachers. Flanders (1960) argues for the distribution rather than centralization of power in the classroom. Pupils have legitimate sources of influence based on interpersonal skills and friendship patterns. If the teacher centralizes the authority too greatly in himself he is likely to arouse tension in the classroom.

Although Flanders argues for less teacher control, the work of Fiedler (1965) on leadership effectiveness in a variety of work groups suggests that the desirable degree of control to be employed by a leader should vary with the favorability of circumstances. Fiedler hypothesized that three important group factors should contribute to leader and group effectiveness: the degree of mutual liking between leader and followers, the extent to which the task is structured, and the degree to which the leader's position is clearly felt to be legitimate.

Fiedler's extensive research using these variables found that when the leader is well liked, the task is highly structured, and the leader's position is clearly felt to be legitimate—all favorable conditions for productivity—a leader tends to be more effective if he is directive and controlling. He is likely to be followed no matter how controlling he gets, since there is little resistance. When the leader is not liked, the task is unstructured, and the leader's legitimacy is in question—all unfavorable conditions—exerting a high degree of control will also be the most effective strategy. Less control will be inadequate to meet the demands of the situation. Where intermediate conditions exist, e.g., good leader-follower relationships, unstructured tasks, and strong or weak leader position, the leadership style which will produce the greatest success will be one which is human-relations-oriented, i.e., more permissive, passive, and considerate. Here cooperation from group members will be required and can be obtained, but submission cannot be counted on.

If we try to apply Fiedler's notions to the school situation, it would seem that when the teacher who is well liked and whose authority is respected is faced with a structured situation, such as organized team sports, he should be more directive, while in an unstructured situation such as free play he should be more oriented to human needs. For the disliked teacher without legitimate authority the opposite strategies should work better; he should use a more directive approach where there is less structure, and a more person-oriented approach where there is more structure.

CONCLUSION

In applying general leadership principles to the teaching situation, one should not lose sight of the distinctive obvious properties of leadership in the classroom. The teacher generally has considerably higher status by virtue of age, education, and academic skills than does the pupil; the teacher is vested with authority over students by society; and the leadership is legitimately directed at certain specific task areas. These are generally highly favorable conditions for assertion of leadership. They break down, however, when either the teacher or pupils fail to accept general societal prescriptions for teacher and pupil roles.

CHAPTER SIX

CONFORMITY AND DEVIANCE IN CLASSROOM GROUPS

It is very common to hear people in our society decry "conformity" and sing chords of praise for the independent or creative individual. Yet for many people, there is a reluctance to recognize the tremendous pressures towards conformity and the disturbing consequences of deviance. These pressures can be seen quite clearly among children. For many if not all of us, recollections of childhood are marred by such phrases as: "Nigger!" "Teacher's pet!" "Bully!" "Four-eyes!" "Fatty!" "Slut!" One of these or similar terms hit many of us "below the belt," recalling terribly painful experiences in school where we were "picked on" by other group members. Where it was only a single other child who threw the epithet in our face and we had supporters on our side, the pain was minimal. If, however, we were alone and open to attack by all other group members, the pain may still be substantial in recall. Why do groups "pick on" individuals? What need is thus served?

There are basically two kinds of explanation which have been offered for reactions to deviant behavior, one based on individual motivations, the other on group needs. The first states that we all have unconscious hostile feelings toward persons to whom we cannot express these feelings, either because it would threaten a desired relationship or because the other might retaliate. These hostile feelings require some outlet and social groups become identified as acceptable targets for individual hostility. This approach has been elaborated considerably in the theory of the "Authoritarian Personality." During and just after World War II, in which six million Jews had been exterminated by Nazi Germany, a group of psychologists carried out a major investigation aimed at discovering the determinants of anti-Semitism. Their major hypothesis was that anti-Semitism is not an isolated phenomenon, but rather is part of a generalized hostility towards minority groups, and that it derives from deep needs within the personality to control the expression of strong hostile impulses. The investigators constructed paper and pencil measures of anti-Semitism, anti-Negro prejudice, and prejudice toward other minority groups. They found these to be closely related to one another: that is, those who were most anti-Semitic tended to be the most strongly anti-Negro and so on. Then a measure was constructed of ethnocentrism, or generally positive feeling towards one's own group and negative feelings towards "outgroups." Finally, a measure was derived of the personality underlying prejudice. The measure, called the "F" (for Fascism) scale, was designed to predict prejudice without mentioning minority groups. The F scale was based on extensive personality interviews and tests on people who had previously scored very low or very high on anti-Semitism. The investigators found these highly prejudiced people to have a distinctive childhood upbringing which included strong parental control of hostile and sexual impulses. These people were, as adults, strongly repressed; that is, they could not accept their own basic impulses, and had a strong need for order and for autocratic relationships. Underlying their controlled exterior lay covert, strong hostile and sexual impulses which the individuals expressed by attributing them to others, particularly those of inferior status or minority group members. Once they saw the outgroup as having these unacceptable characteristics, they felt it appropriate to express strong hostile feelings towards the group.

Let us now shift from the psychodynamic approach to a group dynamics approach. In an investigation by Schachter (1951) groups of students were asked to discuss a juvenile court case and come up with recommendations. The case was slanted to arouse sympathy for the boy, who had come from a very poor home environment. Unknown to the other members of the group, one subject was a confederate of the experimenter. In some groups, the confederate took a consistently *conforming* position. In other groups the confederate took and maintained an unpopular, *deviant* position, favoring a punitive recommendation. Finally, in a third condition, the confederate began as a deviate, but then *gradually changed* his view until it matched the opinion of the other group members. The study showed that the deviate was spoken to more frequently in an attempt to get him to change his position. When group members were asked to choose who they would want as a friend, it was clear that they did not want the deviate. In contrast they did accept the confederate who gradually changed position from deviancy to conformance.

This study is a good demonstration of the pressure a group placed on members to conform and the consequences of nonconformity. Findings of this and other studies indicate that such pressures are greater where the group is cohesive and the issue important to its members.

A series of studies by Solomon Asch (1956) demonstrates the power of group pressures. College students were asked to judge which of three lines matched a comparison line in size. In every case they made their judgment aloud after hearing several others judge the same set of lines. Unknown to the subject, the others in the group were all confederates of the experimenter. On many of the trials, every one of these confederates chose the same obviously incorrect line. The subject, responding after the confederates, frequently went along with the incorrect group consensus despite his ability to clearly distinguish the correct answer. If conformity occurs even when objective data are clearly available to contradict the group opinion, it appears that group pressures can be very effective in forcing compliance. An important finding of later studies, however, was that such conformity disappeared when one other group member also disagreed with the majority. Furthermore, even in the previous experiment, only about 35% of the subjects actually conformed to the confederates' judgments and when conformity did occur it was frequently only public conformity, the individual reporting privately that he did not hold the opinion. These group pressures for conformity are great but not all-powerful. In most cases, where individuals have no strong reasons for opposing all other members of their group, many of them will go along with the others rather than cause dissension.

To summarize the group interpretation: people have a strong need to be members of groups composed of persons holding similar beliefs and showing similar behavior. Whenever possible they put pressure on others to become more similar to themselves or they try to change their own behavior to conform to others. If a person *remains* deviant within the group, he will be disliked and, if possible, rejected from the group. He, in turn, will dislike the group and, if possible, leave it for a more satisfying group.

"DEVIANCE" IN SCHOOL

The compulsory classroom group presents a special problem. Since the child cannot voluntarily leave the classroom group if he deviates from group norms, he must either conform or face a hostile group. And if his deviation is in physique, ethnic background, race, skill, or any other observable and unchangeable characteristic, he has no escape. Often he will be a source of distress to the group and thus will be attacked or isolated from the others. This classroom experience is likely to seriously affect the academic progress as well as the social adjustment of the child. Not only will he feel distaste for the school, but he will tend to focus his attention on the interpersonal classroom conflict rather than on academic work.

Though the emphasis here has been on destructive reactions of groups toward deviant members, there is also some evidence for constructive or protective reactions toward the deviate. Dentler and Erikson (1959) point out that deviant individuals serve important functions for the group, by clarifying group standards and making others feel more accepted. Although this would seem not to help the deviate, it also can be shown that groups will protect such persons from outside dangers with which the individual could not cope. One can think of many illustrations of such behavior by a group to protect its own low status members. Dentler and Erikson describe the reactions of Army recruits toward mentally ill members in their midst. The recruits protected them from the authorities, despite repeated deviance. Similarly, families will often protect their mentally ill, physically handicapped, and mentally retarded members despite great personal cost to other family members.

How common are such reactions in the classroom? One can certainly think of fellow students who cover up for a cheating classmate despite their strong distaste for cheating. The norm for protecting group members against the outsider or authority figure is often stronger, i.e., supported by more powerful sanctions, than the norm against cheating. If the standard, such as "no cheating," is defined by outside authorities, such as teachers, rather than by the members themselves, we are dealing with rule-breaking rather than deviation from group norms. Where standards are set only by teachers, pupil failure to "shape up" may be defined as rebelliousness.

Rebelliousness has received greatest attention in the study of adolescents, particularly in the high school setting. Stinchcombe (1964) in his study *Rebellion in a High School* has attacked previous explanations of adolescent disobedience to school authority. Others hold that the teenager's peer relationships are so important to him that he must concentrate his efforts on conforming to his own group. Since the peer group norms often differ from school norms, the argument continues, the individual's behavior appears deviant to the school administration and teachers. A second set of explanations emphasizes the large number of lower-class teenagers who have learned in their subculture a set of values which does not match the values of the middle-class school. These two forms of behavior seem to deviate almost accidentally from school norms. One could argue that if schools did not follow the norms of middle-class adult society but rather the norms of youth or lower-class adult society, there would be no student deviation from school norms.

In contrast, Stinchcombe proposes an active, intentional, hostile reaction by adolescents against school authorities because the school fails to have any relevance for their future, and fails to provide them with adult privileges that students desire. The adolescent is disturbed and disturbing not because he has unrealistic or immature goals but rather because he is striving toward adulthood and the school fails to help him, blocks his path toward these goals, and denies that the goals are appropriate. He wants to enjoy sex and alcohol, to make important decisions himself; these opportunities are denied him. Also, he wants to be able to get a good job when he finishes school, but he knows that if he is not one of the better academic students, the school will not adequately prepare him for this.

Coleman (1965) has pointed out that even the bright, college-bound pupil in the academically oriented school is poorly motivated to perform academic work. These students are not rebels, however. They are strong conformists to a peer group culture which emphasizes athletics and social life. Coleman asks whether academic material cannot be taught using some of the strong motivations of the adolescent, including his desire to work as a team member instead of competing with his peers for grades, his exhibitionistic desires, and his interest in the "real world" outside the classroom. Coleman suggests that this could be accomplished by teaching through games which simulate real and important personal and social problems.

Both Stinchcombe and Coleman suggest that schools should be modified to satisfy the needs of adolescents rather than trying to shape adolescents to unrealistic or inappropriate demands of the school. Present student rebellion or disobedience may thus be seen as a symptom of inappropriate rules or of a lack of demonstrable legitimacy of the flaunted authority, rather than a symptom of adolescent turmoil or poor adjustment.

One of the explanations given above for rebellious behavior was that it was really conforming behavior, i.e., behavior conforming to peer group demands. The general point to be raised is whether any behavior is "really" independent or deviant. Might not most apparently nonconforming behavior be simply explained by the observer's having looked at the wrong group? We don't change our behavior to fit just any group to which others think we belong. We only try to match our behavior to groups with which we identify, that we like, or that we aspire to. Only such groups form a frame of reference for us. These groups have been called "reference groups."[1] The unkempt, bearded, long-haired young man may seem deviant from his sex, age, and national group. But when we see the people he chooses for friends, we are likely to find that they bear a close resemblance to him.

The special difficulty in identifying this unusual behavior as conforming derives from the value his group places on nonconformity to the large societal norms. A similar problem exists in adolescent rebellion, where peer group norms devalue the norms prescribed by the school. In such cases, the individual's behavior may be adequately explained by his conformity to his reference group. One then needs to ask why his group values nonconformance to larger societal standards. Here the sort of explanations proposed by Stinchcombe for the high school rebel seem very appropriate.

It would be too cynical to claim that all nonconforming behavior can be attributed to the observer's misidentification of the person's reference group. We can all think of instances in which a person takes a solitary stand or breaks new ground with no conceivable social support. He may be able to do this

---

1. See discussion of reference groups in Chapter 7.

because his leadership in the group and conformity to certain norms is so well established that he has picked up "idiosyncrasy credits." He may have no strong group identification or he may be the "inner-directed" man. He does things because they are "right" or "good" or "moral" on the basis of values and norms developed during his childhood. In a sense, he is conforming to a reference group, his family, but the group and its values exist in the past. In the present they are a largely indistinguishable part of his self. A further variant of "conforming nonconformity" is found in groups which have as a norm creative, original behavior—"doing your own thing."

INVOLUNTARY DEVIANCE

Another kind of nonconforming behavior is identified as deviance but not independence, since it is involuntary deviance resulting from uncontrollable personal characteristics such as physical deformities, mental illness, and mental retardation, or less extreme ones such as race or poor athletic or reading skill. Here the "odd" person seems at the mercy of the group. He can't change; thus the group must adjust to him, tolerate him, or discard him. Or he can leave the group voluntarily because of the intolerant and intolerable reactions of group members. But can't he change? Can't he "pass" as one of the group?

Erving Goffman in his book *Stigma* distinguishes between the discreditable and the already discredited individual—between the person whose deviant characteristics are not yet known by others and the one whose deviant features are either immediately visible or have become known.

The discreditable person is concerned with controlling information about himself so that he may pass for normal. For example, the hard-of-hearing teenager who has just moved to a new neighborhood may try to act as if he can hear as well as others in order not to risk rejection by them. This may require such devices as dominating the conversation, avoiding people who talk softly, or admitting ignorance or poor preparation when asked questions by the teacher. The problem of controlling information about his defect can dominate such a child's attention. He has to be alert for cues to which he should be responding and always ready to avoid a situation in which his disability may be disclosed. In the long run, even if he is "passing," he may prefer to disclose his stigma to reduce the tremendous tension he is experiencing. He then becomes a discredited individual and faces a somewhat different set of problems, similar to those of any individual with a visible defect. He must now concentrate on "covering," or minimizing the socially disturbing aspects of his disability.

Beatrice Wright in her book *Physical Disability—A Psychological Approach* has focused on the "overlapping situations" in which the disabled person finds himself. He sees himself as a member of the normal group and also as a handicapped person. His dilemma is that if he acts in a normal way, he may "pass" or manage the interpersonal tension, but if he is discovered to be ineffective in carrying out the normal role, he may be discredited, embarrassed, or rejected. This may occur, for example, with a blind person if he does not take into account his limitations when some special physical adjustment or help is required, as in identifying a street in a new neighborhood. On the other hand, if he acts handicapped and "keeps his place," as would a blind teenager in a school for the blind, he avoids traumatic situations but tends to feel devalued and misses certain privileges of the normal person. In the school situation, it would not be unexpected to find students who refuse to admit a vision or hearing problem because it is viewed as a stigma, and they fear it would result in their being devalued by their peers. However, trying to cope without help may result in the child's responding inappropriately to questions or requests and being seen as retarded by the teacher and stupid by his peers.

The mentally ill and the retarded face special problems because their deviant characteristic involves poor adjustment skills.

Their family members or teachers may try to "cover" for them or manage tension-arousing situations for them. The parent wants to "pass" as a normal mother or father and also may be protecting the child's self-esteem. Unless very young or severely retarded or severely mentally ill, the child will be aware of his special status with others. Thus adolescents in institutions for the retarded or mentally ill are continually denying that they belong with the others. Patients in such "hospitals" frequently explain that they were put in for committing a crime and not because they were "crazy" or mentally retarded. In many cases they are correct. Such institutions are used for two kinds of patients: the helpless patient who is too disturbed or retarded to care for himself, and the patient who has caused social problems in the community. Fortunately, improved services within the community are becoming available for the less severely retarded and disturbed. Fewer persons are having to undergo what Goffman (1962) has called the "mortification of the self" in being socialized into the large residential institution. Such institutions have obviously functioned to handle the "rejects" of the larger society and have treated them as less than human, removing their normal privileges, including their personal property, clothing, freedom of movement and, in general, all those characteristics which go to make up the person's notion of his self. These are sacrificed on the altar of efficiency and economy, which require production-line handling of large groups of inmates.

Recent trends to get the retarded and mentally ill out of institutions have not always improved things for such persons. They now have to compete in a world where they are at the bottom. The problem is not so bad for those who were never inside. For those who have a record, the consequence may be severe. Not only have they been forced to adjust to an atypical environment which provided little training or incentive for individual coping, but they have been labeled, stigmatized as retarded. If such a person behaves inadequately on the job and in his relationships with others—in short, if he cannot "make it" in his community—it may be because he is retarded or because of his social history and the manner in which people have labeled him.

In these as well as other types of deviance, it may be difficult to separate initial deviance from socially induced deviance. Once you have been identified as different, others define a new role for you; they expect different things from you and place different demands on you, which in turn is likely to alter your behavior so that you fit the role, i.e., your behavior resembles the expectations more closely.

The case of the institutionalized deviate may be more dramatic than the way in which deviates are treated in the community and in public schools, but it is a difference in degree and not in kind. Deviant roles and role expectations are also created for the mentally retarded and problem child in the public schools, both in segregated classes and within the regular classes. In what seems at first to be a beneficial situation, a child thought to be retarded may be given less challenging tasks by the teacher. While this protects the child from failure, it may reduce his opportunity to learn. This was illustrated in the Beez (1968) study with preschool children referred to in Chapter 1. Similarly, a child identified as emotionally disturbed may be "protected" from the normal social demands of peer groups, yet it may be just this social pressure which might better control and modify his behavior.

Though these consequences of teacher role expectations for the disturbed and retarded child may seem only slight in the short run, in the long run the child may become completely socialized to the role. He will act retarded and will not take intellectual risks, because he thinks he is retarded and because he has been trained only to a level of competence expected of retarded children. If he has learned the role "emotionally disturbed" well, he will avoid others, whom he has not had to learn to cope with, or he may feel no reservation about expressing his hostile impulses since his teachers have "taught" him that he is disturbed and therefore cannot keep himself from expressing his impulses.

A good illustration of an arrangement in the public schools which fosters the development of a deviant role is the special class for the "educable mentally retarded" child (IQ approximately 60-80). These classes are justified on two grounds: (1) the need of the retarded child for specialized attention and (2) the finding that the retarded child is often poorly accepted by his normal classmates.

The consequences of this segregation of the mildly retarded is that while they feel more adequate relative to their new classmates, they are even more likely to be seen as deviant by teachers and other pupils in school. The special class has labeled them and reduced the likelihood that they can ever again pass as normal while in school. There is considerable evidence that most of these children were not identified as deviant or subnormal *before* they entered school and are not seen as subnormal once they leave school (Guskin and Spicker, 1968). The school's demands and diagnostic facilities define the child as retarded.

Another argument in support of segregated arrangements for "retarded" students is that it allows the individualized teaching which will foster the child's achievement. Several studies have examined the academic achievement consequences of special class placement and these investigations demonstrate no superiority of achievement for retarded students in special classes over those remaining in regular classes. In fact, whatever differences are found favor the regular class retarded child. This is consistent with Beez's finding of the influence of negative teacher expectations, which is to reduce the demands placed on a "low ability" child and thus reduce the performance level of the child. In short, the special class seems to create and stabilize a "retarded" social role for its pupils. Similar results can be expected for low ability tracks. Here children expected not to succeed are given teachers and a curriculum which preclude success and foster dropping out of school.

The general principle to be derived here is that demanding uniformity not only fosters conformity but also institutionalizes deviance. Groups identify persons who differ in some way, and if the individual cannot "shape up," he is relegated to a special group or special position in the group with different expectations from those of other group members. These role expectations then encourage others to treat him differently, which in turn creates new deviant behavior which fulfills the expectations.

However, some groups have considerable tolerance for a wide range of individual behaviors. They may even support individual members' "self expression," creativity, and uniqueness by rewarding openness and originality. Under such conditions, conforming to the group norms does not result in uniformity but in diversity.

Similarly, the teacher, by virtue of his power, may lead students either to match narrowly stated demands or to come up with creative answers. Restatements of a teacher's own words may be rejected by such a teacher and well-thought-out disagreements may be rewarded. It becomes a question of matching basic values (i.e., creativity) rather than matching specific behaviors (i.e., the "right" answer).

CHAPTER SEVEN

THE SCHOOL AND THE SOCIALIZATION OF YOUTH

INTRODUCTION

Socialization is the process by which an individual learns the behaviors, the values, and the expectations of others that enable him to take on particular roles in society. Individuals are not born with skills that enable them to function in particular types of roles. We have only to see the behavior of a recently arrived immigrant, when he attempts to function in the roles of his adopted country, to know that such roles are learned.

Indicative of the problems of an immigrant are his difficulty in understanding or communicating in the new language, his ignorance of the commonly accepted patterns of interpersonal interaction, his inability to predict the expectations that others have for him, and his behaving in a manner that fails to provide cues for others to understand what to expect of him. These four elements of role behavior—language, norms, others' expectations, behavioral cues to others—are all interrelated and are all essential if an individual is to function effectively in the institutions of society, whether it be as student, teacher, politician, physician, or factory worker (see the earlier discussion of roles in Chapter 1).

The immigrant often comes abruptly face to face with these problems for which he has little preparation, while the native-born child usually acquires these skills at an early age and continues to develop them throughout his life. We usually think of this learning process as occurring within the family,[1] but the example of the immigrant who eventually learns how to take on meaningful societal roles, or in other words becomes socialized, points out the importance of other types of socialization institutions in society. The immigrant child goes to school and learns the language and desired behaviors of his new country; the immigrant adult similarly learns these skills but through training-on-the-job or in such social agencies as settlement houses, community centers, religious organizations. In a similar, though less intense, manner a native-born child refines his skills in nonfamily institutions such as the school or the community center, which enable him to test his behavior with other youth as well as "socialized" adults other than his parents.

There is usually considerable similarity or congruence between the values and norms of the two major socialization agencies, the family and the school. In such situations, the socialization function of the school seems to be to clarify and develop the student's societally relevant skills and self-expectations and to make sure they are related to society's expectations of him.

However, when there is a lack of congruence between clear and consistent norms and values of the dominant culture and those of the youth of a particular group in society, the school is in effect commissioned by society with the role of influencing these youth to learn the new norms and values, that is, to resocialize the students. A good example of this is the aforementioned case of immigrant youth.

A very different situation exists for the school's role in educating students if there is confusion about the accepted

---

1   The socialization literature, reflecting the influence of Freud and personality theory, strongly emphasizes the parent-child relationship. See Zigler and Child (1969).

values and desired behaviors. When teachers and school personnel are faced with contradictory and relatively distinct sets of desirable norms and values, they may be unable to "resocialize" or even adequately socialize their students. Such contradictory pressures on the school as a socializing institution seem to be particularly great in times of rapid social change.

At present, the schools are finding it difficult to act as socialization agents for Negro youth. This confusion permeates many aspects of school life and makes it very difficult for us to see the socialization processes at work. Some insight into the nature of these processes may be obtained from a study of school resocialization practices for immigrant youth in a highly centralized society that has clear and strong norms and values which penetrate directly into the school setting. Later in this chapter we present such a situation, in which the school system of Thailand has a clear mission to assimilate (i.e., resocialize) Chinese youth. In that analysis we try to bring into bold relief the student-teacher and, to a lesser degree, the student-student interpersonal processes that are common, in drastically modified forms, to most school socialization settings.

This introduction to the topic of socialization has emphasized a number of points:

1) Socialization is the process by which individuals learn skills which enable them to perform useful roles in the future.

2) The training of youth to take on these future roles occurs in *at least* two major social institutions—the family and the school.

3) As the needs of society are constantly evolving and changing, the socialization practices of schools must change to meet these needs.

4) During periods of rapid social change schools are usually subject to contradictory demands which they must resolve, although they usually are ill equipped to do so.

5) The school can be seen as a developmental socialization institution which clarifies and builds upon the family's

child-rearing practices, and/or as a resocialization institution attempting radical change in the skills and self-expectations of youth (e.g., immigrant youth).

The socialization process is continuous throughout an individual's life. While the foundation for future behaviors may be laid in the early years of childhood and adolescence, the individual is constantly taking on new roles for which he has little or no preparation, a radically new job, for example, or the role of husband-father, wife-mother. To be effective in the new situation he will have to be socialized through training or through the more difficult conditions of trial and error learning while participating in his new role. In the future, as rapid social changes make early socialization experiences less relevant to the needs of the society, more structured adult socialization settings may have to be developed to assure the competence of individuals to perform new roles.[2]

This chapter will be devoted to an analysis of the above five points with special references to (1) the relationships between the family and school socialization experiences for Negro youth, (2) the role of the school in the resocialization (i.e., assimilation) of immigrant youth, and (3) the processes of socialization at the college level.

RELATIONSHIP BETWEEN FAMILY AND SCHOOL SOCIALIZATION

Achievement Orientation

Since one of our continuing interests throughout this book has been the low-income Negro student and his relationship to school, it seems fitting that we delve into the effects of his family's socialization practices on his ability to perform in

---

2   See Donald Michael's *The Unprepared Society* (1968) on the future needs for retraining of adults as society changes.

school. One important theory is that the Negro family situation does not create a high need for achievement in their children.

McClelland (1961), Atkinson (1964), and their associates have carried out a large number of research projects on achievement motivation in a number of different countries and in the United States. Almost all of their research in the United States has been carried out on white male subjects, but they feel that their findings are also applicable to Negro Americans. The need to achieve is seen as a relatively stable and general feature of personality that impels individuals to strive for success whenever their performance at a task can be evaluated against a standard of excellence. Atkinson (1964) states, "The disposition called achievement motive might be conceived as a capacity for taking pride in accomplishment when success at one or another activity is achieved" (p. 241).

To investigate the development of this motive or disposition, a number of psychologists have studied the manner in which parents behave toward their children. Winterbottom (1958) developed measures for investigating the extent to which parents' desires and behavior operate in a way which emphasizes their children's self-mastery of the environment and their achievement. The results indicate that children with a high need for achievement come from homes in which parents said they trained them for self-mastery and achievement at an earlier age than was typical of low achievement-oriented youth. Observing the behavior of fathers and mothers, a number of researchers have come to the following conclusions (Winterbottom, 1958, Rosen, 1962): that (1) high need achieving boys had mothers inclined to give approval (e.g., hugging and kissing) when the child's performance was good and to criticize them when their efforts did not come up to acceptable standards; (2) mothers and fathers of boys with a high need for achievement typically set higher standards for their sons than did other parents; (3) strong control of a boy by his father seems to be especially inhibiting for his achievement motivation—that is, father dominance inhibits the boy's desire for independent achievement.

As a result of early achievement-oriented child-rearing practices, children develop a desire to master their environment and to meet rather high standards of excellence. These standards are, in childhood, set by their parents or other significant individuals in their environment. When they attend school these standards are set by their teachers and peers. No matter what "significant other persons" set the standards of excellence, the high achievement-oriented person will, it seems, strive toward these accepted goals.

McClelland (1961) maintains that the home experiences of many low-income Negro youth inhibit the development of high achievement striving. Of particular importance, he feels, are the mother-oriented family (particularly when there is no father present) and the strong dependence of the child on his mother. It would seem that the combination of the dependence and the fact that many of the mothers have to work and thus be away from the children may reduce the tendency for mothers to set standards of excellence.

However, one should be cautious in making such an analysis. While low-income Negro youth may have a lower need for achievement than middle-class youth (this has not been substantiated in any significant way), the mother-oriented family situation is not necessarily the causal factor. Mothers could set the standards of excellence and reward patterns necessary for the development of a strong achievement orientation. The absence of a father does not necessarily mean that the interpersonal processes between parent and child that lead to a high achievement motive will not occur. Again, the fact that certain processes produce high need for achievement in families in which both mother and father are present does not mean that a situation in which there is only a mother will produce a lack of the behaviors typical of fathers. The mother in such situations may take on new responsibilities. In short, whether a fatherless home will create a high or low achievement orientation in the children is a question to be answered by research. As of the present, no such research seems available.

Moreover, some recent research indicates that the situation in which a person finds himself may produce a high need for achievement even if the child-rearing practices of his home would seem to have created the conditions leading to a low achievement orientation. Veroff, Feld, and Gurin (1962) report that Catholic men—who, due to family organization (e.g., father dominance), were expected to have a lower need for achievement than Protestants—actually had a higher achievement orientation. One reason for this might be that the generally lower-income Catholic fathers had a great need to support their families, and therefore tended to work extremely hard. Thus they showed a high need for achievement because such strivings fulfilled a basic value, the importance of supporting one's family and making it secure.

While the research on achievement motivation has spanned two decades and has accumulated an extremely large number of studies, there are some social psychologists (e.g., Katz, 1967) who have serious misgivings about its implications, especially its usefulness in understanding the problem of the under-achievement of Negro youth in the classroom. Is the achievement motive of a particular individual aroused equally in sports, classrooms, and dating situations? We have almost no research to support such a conclusion. Katz (1967) states that even if low-income Negro youth are low in need achievement, "the lower class Negro pupil's disinterest in classroom learning may be less a matter of his lacking the achievement motive than of its being directed into nonintellectual pursuits" (p. 144). If such is the case, is it not possible that the classroom situation has "turned off" the low-income Negro student while the athletic field has not? May we not then ask what teacher-student learning relationship might stimulate these youth? The problem may be less the fault of the student and more the result of the school and classroom atmosphere. The student may also be sensing the irrelevance of classroom learning for his future.

Educational Values and Skills
One common explanation for the poor achievement of Negro students is that their parents do not instill in them a feeling for

the value of education and a desire for it. The assumption is that, because these youths do not perform well in school, they and their parents really lack the desire for such achievement. A number of research studies seem to indicate that this assumption is inaccurate. In two studies (Bell, 1965, and Keller, 1963) a majority of upper-lower class (i.e., working class) Negro parents wanted their sons to have a college education and conveyed these aspirations to their children as expectations to be fulfilled. Other studies indicate that Negro students do have such aspirations (e.g., Coleman *et al.,* 1966).

Yet, the reality of the performance of these students seems to indicate that such aspirations are in the realm of wishful thinking. The question that emerges is, given these educational aspirations, why don't low-income Negro students perform better in schools? The answer to this question may lie in a number of different directions: (1) the skills of the students to implement these aspirations, (2) the nature of their teachers' behavior toward and expectations of them, and (3) the recognition of the lack of opportunities for fulfillment of aspirations. We shall deal with the first of these in this section and discuss the others in the following sections.

Katz (1967) states that one of the major problems of low-income Negro students is the discrepancy between their educational aspirations and the skills that would enable them to reach such goals.[3] He further states (p. 174) that:

. . . one can hold achievement values and standards that do not get reflected in actual achievement efforts. Values and goals have been internalized, but not the behavioral mechanisms requisite for attaining them. The [lack of congruence between] conditions and behaviors is not difficult to understand, for verbal attitudes are relatively easy to acquire through mere imitation of verbalizations observed in adult or peer models. If the attitudes expressed are the "correct" ones, i.e., are held by

---

3   See the Hess and Shipman (1965) laboratory study which showed that low-income mothers were less effective than middle-class mothers in teaching learning tasks to their children.

socializing agents (the student's parents and teachers)... they will tend to get reinforced either directly or vicariously. But performing the behaviors that are instrumental for attaining the goals is a more difficult feat than the acquisition of verbal attitudes about the goal, especially when there are no models of competency to imitate, and when achievement strivings are not socially recognized and reinforced. Apparently, the typical Negro mother tries to socialize her child for scholastic achievement by laying down verbal rules and regulations about classroom conduct, coupled with punishment of detected transgressions. But she does not do enough to guide and encourage her child's efforts at verbal-symbolic mastery.[4]

Educational aspirations which seem unrealistic in the face of a lack of achievement may, in part, provide the basis for negative self-evaluations by low-income Negro youngsters. The student has high standards which he cannot meet. It is possible that the standards are so stringent and rigid as to be utterly dysfunctional. Thus the child has been socialized to self-imposed failure. It should be noted that in situations where socializing agents—parents, teachers, etc.—are extremely severe in their punishment, the youth may totally withdraw or be openly hostile rather than imitate adult standards.

The Teacher's Contribution to Student Failure

The above analysis indicates that when low-income Negro students enter school they are predisposed to see themselves as failures, even though they desire a high level of education. They lack the skills to succeed. Questions arise about the extent to which the teacher-student relationship leads to the development of these needed skills, or to what degree the teacher reinforces the student's potential negative self-evaluation.

The teacher is potentially a very powerful socializing agent. The very young student, whether black or white, is very dependent

---

4   I. Katz, The socialization of academic motivation in minority group children. In D. Levine (Ed.), *Nebraska Symposium on Motivation* XV, 133-191 (1967), p. 174. Copyright © 1967, University of Nebraska Press.

on the adults in his environment and looks to the teacher for direction. This dependence is intensified by the teacher's clear authority over his future. Moreover, previously cited research on the effects of the expectations of important others (see the discussion in Chapters 1 and 2) suggests that teachers can cause significant changes in the student's intellectual performance and self-expectations. Thus the young student's self-evaluation can be altered by the expectations of his teacher, his warmth, his approval, his annoyance. This probably occurs because of the newness of the classroom situation and the student's uncertainty about his ability to succeed. The teacher offers him new information about himself, thereby influencing his uncertainty and anxiety about his competence—whether it be positive or negative.

It would seem that the effect of this teacher influence should be related to the student's previous experiences of success and failure in and outside the school. Thus we would expect a middle-class white child who has received considerable support and positive reinforcement of his intellectual abilities to be less influenced by the teacher's expectations. On the other hand, we would expect that a child who has received little positive (or negative) reinforcement to be most susceptible to his teacher's view of him. From the previous discussion of the low-income Negro child it would seem that he not only lacks the skill to achieve but also, at best, has received few rewards or positive reinforcements for learning or achievement striving in a classroom type of situation. Therefore, we would expect him to be very susceptible to his teacher's expectations of his performance. Some research on the attitudes, impressions, and expectations of teachers about Negro students strikes a very depressing note.

In an attempt to assess the difference in reactions of teachers to low-income Negro and middle-class white youth, Judith Guskin (1968) presented separate groups of student-teachers with a tape recording of the speech of a middle-class white child and a low-income Negro child. Each group was asked a series of questions about what they had heard. While the words of the two children were exactly the same, the differences in the speech of these two youths led the teachers to assess them very differently. The Negro child was thought to be less intelligent, to score much lower on achievement tests, to have a bleak future (e.g., be a school drop-out), to participate in disruptions and, in general, to come from a "culturally deprived" background.

Thus, when only the language of the child—not his behaviors, dress, or any other characteristic—was considered, the future teachers expected him to be a failure in school. While this study dealt only with the attitudes of the student-teachers, it would seem to be a good guess that such attitudes would be operative in the classroom.

Another study (Henriott and St. John, 1966) interviewed a nationwide sample of teachers and principals in urban public schools. They found that schools with a student population from the lowest socioeconomic levels had a racial composition of over 70% Negro and less than 30% white. A larger proportion of the teachers at such schools than at schools with students who were white and from higher socioeconomic levels were said to enjoy work less, to be less loyal to their principal, to desire transfer to other schools, and to have less favorable opinions of the motivation and behavior of their students. Principals in such schools stated that they had a smaller proportion of teachers who were competent, who tried to improve their competence, or who were strongly interested in their students. This study indicates that Negro students, who make up most of the student population of these "lower-class" schools, were subjected to a larger number of incompetent teachers who resented teaching and who, it would seem, encouraged in their students tendencies towards debilitating self-criticisms.

Katz (1967) summarizes some of the literature on the effects of teachers on Negro students and states the following:

[The teachers'] influence on Negro students' motivation may be considerable, particularly in the lower elementary grades when children are more emotionally dependent on adults.

Apparently, many teachers inadvertently dispense strong nega-
tive reinforcements in the form of personal disapproval and
rejection, and studies of teachers' attitudes towards lower-class
pupils suggest that the incidence of such teachers in pre-
dominantly Negro schools is relatively high. The effect on the
dependent Negro child is likely to be a strengthening of his
tendency toward indiscriminate self-derogation of his own
learning efforts.[5]

The teachers' negative expectations of their Negro students'
performance in class and the manner in which they create or
support the students own negative self-evaluations may explain
the debilitating effects of track systems. Because Negro students
often find themselves in the "slow" classes, possibly as the
result of the built-in discrimination of intelligence tests or the
prejudice of teachers, they are faced with teachers who expect
them to be poor students, to be unmotivated, and the like. As a
result of the students' acceptance of this label they confirm
their teachers' expectations by behaving poorly. Thus the
"prophecy" of poor achievement fulfills itself. The expectations, the poor achievement, and the negative self-evaluations continue to reinforce each other. Therefore, students
who may have entered school with high educational aspirations
and a lack of skills to achieve these goals over time learn that
they are not and will never be competent to succeed in a school
setting. The track system plays into this self-fulfilling prophecy
by not permitting the student to gain a sense of his own
competence to perform adequately in school. Thus the teacher
expects failure, the students accept their own failure, and the
teacher is therefore "justified" in not attempting to teach them.
If this is true, it is a terrible indictment of our urban school
systems.

Evidence that the relative academic status of these students
actually becomes worse as they move through school is
presented in the studies by Deutsch and his colleagues (1965).

---

5 I. Katz, The socialization of academic motivation in minority group
children. In D. Levine (Ed.), *Nebraska Symposium on Motivation* XV,
133-191 (1967), p. 178. Copyright © 1967, University of Nebraska Press.

While Negro students enter school *slightly less* competent than their white peers, by the time they reach the sixth grade the achievement scores of the Negro students have become *much worse* than their white counterparts. Clark (1965) amplifies this:

> . . . *the data here presented show that the major deterioration in learning takes place between the third and sixth grades, not in the first and second grades. This leads to the inference that underachievement is the result of an accumulation of deficiencies while in school, rather than the result of deficiencies prior to school.*[6]

Perceived Opportunities

An important factor affecting students as they move through school is their perception of the success of other people like them and of the potential opportunities available to them in the larger society. One of the major motivating factors for learning is the realization that present success is relevant for the future.

As was mentioned above, Negro youth seem to have high educational aspirations. In a recent series of studies, Patricia Gurin and her colleagues (1969) point out that Negro youth and adults have adopted the general cultural belief that an individual's success is contingent upon his own work and behavior. However, they also report that Negroes feel that these beliefs cannot always be applied in their own personal life situations.

The authors have come to this conclusion from their research on the extent to which Negro and white individuals perceive that they have control over their own fate or the extent to which they perceive rewards as contingent on their own behavior (internal control) as against the extent to which they see their fate as controlled by forces outside themselves and

---

6   K. B. Clark, *Dark Ghetto: Dilemmas of Social Power.* New York: Harper & Row, 1967, p. 139. Quoted by permission of the publisher.

occurring independently of their own actions (external control).[7] These notions of fate control (internal and external) can be looked at from two perspectives; beliefs about one's own *personal* life, and beliefs about people in general (i.e., cultural beliefs or ideology).[8] Gurin and her associates (1969) found differences in the manner in which Negro and white students view their personal fate control but not their cultural beliefs.

Without the same experiences of discrimination and racial prejudice[as Negroes], whites are less likely to perceive an inconsistency between cultural beliefs and what works for them. [On the other hand] Negro students may endorse general cultural beliefs in the Protestant Ethic (i.e., internal control or ability to control one's own fate) just as strongly as would their white peers; at the same time, they may express much less certainty that they can control the outcomes of their own lives.[9]

An example of the cultural belief/internal control statement on which both Negro and white college students respond in the same manner is "If people are not successful, it is their own fault." A personal/external control statement on which there are different reactions by Negro and white students is "Every time I try to get ahead, something or somebody stops me." Negroes tend to agree with this statement while whites tend to disagree. Hence, in general, Negroes as compared to whites have a more external control orientation in their *personal* feelings

---

7   A statement representing internal control is "When I make plans, I am almost certain I can make them work." The external control opposite of this is "It is not always wise to plan too far ahead because many things turn out to be a matter of good or bad fortune anyhow."

8   An example of a statement that represents personal/internal control is "When I make plans I am almost certain I can make them work." An example of ideology/internal control is "People will get ahead in life if they have the goods to do a good job; knowing the right people has nothing to do with it."

9   P. Gurin, G. Gurin, R. C. Lao, and M. Beattie, Internal-external control in the motivational dynamics of Negro youth, *Journal of Social Issues* XXV (3), p. 42 (1969). Quoted by permission of the publisher.

about themselves, but they are similar to whites in that their *cultural beliefs* have an internal control orientation.

Of importance from an educational standpoint is that personal and cultural beliefs about control are differentially related to motivation. Gurin, *et al* report that "It is the personal, rather than the ideological, measure that operates significantly in motivation. . . " Therefore, those "students who have a high sense of personal control over their own lives (internal control) also express heightened expectancies of success and self confidence about their abilities for academic and job performance; they also aspire to jobs that are more prestigeful, demanding, and realistic in terms of their own abilities and interests, three characteristics of job aspirations that have been related to high achievement motivation in many studies in the achievement literature" (p. 43). No relationship was found between the ideological orientation and these three motivational characteristics. One conclusion that can be extrapolated from these findings is that since Negro youth *generally* seem to believe in the Protestant ethic (i.e., internal control oriented in cultural beliefs) but seriously question their own ability to control their personal lives (i.e., external control oriented on a personal level) they more than likely will tend to have *lower* expectations about their abilities for academic and job success than their white peers and probably perform more poorly as a result.

An important point which we would like to emphasize at this time is that these expectations are probably realistic given the opportunities available, past and present, for Negro youth. These youth have accepted as a good thing the importance of responsibility and work in order to achieve desirable goals but have come to realize that it doesn't apply to them personally because of the discrimination and racial prejudice in society. This discrimination and prejudice is often reflected in the schools the youths attend, thereby supporting their views about white society.

A further indication of the lack of opportunity for the low-income Negro youth is the dearth of successful academic models in his own school and among community members. The sports and entertainment fields provide models for nonintellectual opportunities but rarely is the ghetto student faced with school-relevant success stories. In fact, the reverse seems to be true. Case after case can be (and probably is) cited by the students' parents and neighbors of high school and college educated Negroes unable to find decent jobs.

Moreover, the people who do succeed in the ghetto are often involved in illegal activities. It is the dope pusher, the person in the numbers racket, and others of this type, who most readily achieve one of the main goals of Americans—to make a lot of money (see Cloward and Ohlin, 1960). While times are changing, it is still probably true that many Negro men who attempt to advance through the legitimate means available in predominantly white America quickly find out that most of these avenues are closed to them. It was, and to a great extent is, only the very exceptional Negro who made it. This lack of past and present opportunities is very apparent to Negro youth. Is it any wonder that many of the average high school students view the academic route with some suspicion?

The discussion presented thus far in this chapter has focused on a number of important concepts—the role of the school and family in the achievement motivation of youth, the difference between educational aspirations and the instrumental skills to achieve such goals, the powerful effects of teachers' expectations on youth and how they discourage low-income black youth, and the effects of a lack of educational and occupational opportunity on students' self-expectations. These factors, among others, are all related to the success of the school and other societal institutions in socializing students to take on adult roles.

RESOCIALIZATION OF IMMIGRANT YOUTH

While schools presented are having a great deal of difficulty redefining goals for adequate and meaningful education, particularly for black youth, the role of schools in times of rapid social change has not always been so confused. Among the major reasons for the inability of schools to change their present direction or reorient themselves are the contradictory demands to which they are being subjected—demands, on the one hand, of the conservative white community for segregated and control-oriented Negro schools and, on the other, from the Negro community for quality education with a black orientation. Moderate community members probably are also divided on these questions. The urban school is thus a battleground for ideological factions, with its own staff split on the best direction in which to move.

At an earlier time in American history, rapid social changes were met with a more consistent and coherent policy. The immigration of a great number of Europeans at the turn of the century created the need for the large-scale reeducation (i.e., resocialization) of immigrant youth. The major responsibility for making these changes was given to the schools. It was their job to create an American identity[10] in the immigrant youth as well as to provide them with the skills that would enable them to become effective adult members of society. The general consensus seems to be that the schools were largely successful—whether their students were the highly educational-oriented European Jews or the peasant groups from Italy or Ireland. Gordon (1964) writes:

... we may note here that in whatever contest ensued between the behavior models of the parents' culture and those of the general American society (the latter pressed upon the new generation's sensibilities by the public school system and the mass media of communication) there was no question as to

---

10 Developing an American national identity did not preclude the maintenance of an identity with an ethnic group. In fact, in many ways the schools tried to maintain the ethnic identity while creating a new national identity. The difference between the two types of identities is best seen in the second-generation Americans (children of immigrants) who are Jewish-Americans, Italian-Americans, and so on.

which would be the winner. In fact, the problem was that the forces were so unevenly balanced that the greater risk consisted in possible alienation from family ties and in status and role reversals of the generations which could easily subvert normal relationships of parents and child.[11]

Another study of Polish immigrants in Australia (Taft and Johnston, 1967) also points out the tremendous influence of the school as compared to the family setting. Delving deeper into the processes by which schools resocialize immigrant youth, Guskin (1968) studied the very successful attempt of the secondary school system of Thailand to resocialize Chinese youth. The rather clear and overt attempts by the Thai secondary school to assimilate Chinese youth present us with a good opportunity to analyze the processes at work in trying to change early socialization patterns. The Thai schools were more ambitious than the educational systems in the United States or Australia; they attempted to change the Chinese into Thais. Not only did they want the Chinese youth to identify as Thai citizens (i.e., national identity), they also attempted to totally detach them from any continuing ethnic identity as Chinese. This attempt was directly supported by Thai society and the Thai governmental policies. If a Chinese became Thai, spoke the Thai language as a Thai, looked like and acted like a Thai,[12] he was given all the occupational and educational opportunities that were open to people born in Thai families. However, if the Chinese students remained Chinese, most of these opportunities were denied to them.

Thus the Thai schools were attempting to change the students' national identity as well as their ethnic identity. To accomplish this the students had first to be disassociated from Chinese influence that would reinforce their attachment to a Chinese identity. In a sense the Thai schools, whether consciously or

---

11 M. Gordon, *Assimilation in American Life.* New York: Oxford University Press, 1964, p. 107. Quoted by permission of the publisher.

12 The Thais and Chinese are not very different in physical appearance.

not, were desocializing the Chinese students; that is, they were attempting to detach them from the conception of themselves that they had learned (been socialized to) as young children. The manner in which the Thai schools have been carrying out the desocialization process is as follows:

1) *Ignoring Chinese culture.* The Thai schools almost totally ignore the Chinese background of their students and actively discourage any discussion of Chinese culture in the school.

2) *Ignorance of language.* The schools require all students to learn the Thai language and severely restrict any use of the Chinese language. This causes a lack of facility in Chinese by the Chinese students. Limiting their contact with the Chinese language to their family and neighborhood leads to a relatively unsophisticated spoken language and little facility in the written language. Moreover, since there are five major Chinese languages besides Mandarin, the language most often taught in Chinese schools, these youth have great difficulty communicating with others who are not in their own language groups. This leads to a greater use of Thai even in communicating with other Chinese students.

3) *Lack of Chinese role models.* The school teachers, who often play the important function of being models for students' behavior, are Thai and not Chinese. Hence the Chinese youth have no adult Chinese role models at the institution in which they spend most of their waking hours. Moreover, the students who are successful in school are those who can succeed in the Thai setting, who speak and behave as Thai. Thus Chinese peer role models are also not readily accessible.

4) *Withdrawal of rewards.* The Chinese youth are not given rewards in accordance with previously learned and desired behaviors. Many behaviors desired in the home are not considered desirable at school.

5) *Punishment—social disapproval.* The Chinese youth are punished in school for behavior considered appropriate at home, and to some extent are reprimanded at home for behavior considered desirable at school. This disagreement

between the two patterns of rewards and punishments seems to be a rather good example of interrole conflict—youth as student and as son or daughter. This conflict would seem to occur even if parents wanted to give their children a Thai education. Since the parents are Chinese they would naturally support Chinese behaviors.

6) *Changing name.* One of the most direct acts of desocialization is the attempt by the schools to persuade the Chinese youth to legally change their names. All Chinese students are encouraged to take on Thai names, and in one secondary school almost 60% did so prior to or during the first year. Considering the importance of the family name in Chinese society, this represents a significant event.

7) *Wearing a uniform.* Since all school children in Thailand wear uniforms, the commonality of dress further intensifies the desired commonality of behavior and identity. This is another way in which the Chinese youth are unable to differentiate themselves from the Thai.

Through these desocialization processes, the Thai schools predispose the Chinese student to change his identity from Chinese to Thai. In effect these desocialization pressures disorient the Chinese child by making him unsure of his feelings about himself and his own ethnic group. The Thai schools use a number of other processes which might be called resocialization pressures in an attempt to create in the student a new conception of himself as Thai, on the basis of new learning and experiences. Three types of resocialization pressures can be specified: the role of the student, the role and power of the teacher, and the power of the school.[13]

---

13 It should be noted that most of the desocialization pressures continue throughout all the secondary school years. Thus, while the desocialization and resocialization pressures are analytically separable, they continually interact with each other throughout the years the Chinese students spend in Thai secondary schools.

As has been maintained by Brim (1966), an attempt to change the behavior and attitudes of individuals requires that their role be clearly and precisely specified. Such definition of role will enable the students to be completely aware of the desired changes and thereby be in a position to perform these behaviors. This requires that there be specific "dos and don'ts," that there be considerable social interaction between the students and the transmitters of these new behaviors (older students and teachers), and that there be ample opportunities for the students to test out their new behaviors.

These role requirements were very much present in Thai schools, especially at one school intensively observed over a nine-month period (Guskin, 1968). Some of the desired Thai behaviors that were clearly distinguished from the undesirable Chinese behaviors were the following:

Desired (Thai)	Undesired (Chinese)
1. Speak quietly, slowly, and softly.	1. Speak rather loudly and harshly.
2. Walk in a slow gait.	2. Walk quickly and with little poise.
3. Be "cool" and calm.	3. Be emotional and aggressive.
4. Speak Thai without an accent.	4. Speak Thai with a heavy accent.

Nevertheless, awareness of these desired behaviors and even the opportunity to perform them may not alone be sufficient. Also of importance is the role and power of the teacher. Brim (1966) maintains that

. . . it appears that if society is to undertake basic resocialization of adults in respect to motives and values, it might well institutionalize in some form the higher power and affectivity relationship characteristic of childhood learning.[14]

---

14   G. O. Brim, Jr., Socialization through the life cycle. In G. O. Brim, Jr., and S. Wheeler, *Socialization After Childhood.* New York: John Wiley & Sons, 1966, p. 37. Quoted by permission of the publisher.

The role of the teacher potentially seems to have such power. He has control over day-to-day affective rewards (approval) and punishments (disapproval) in the classroom as well as the formal power of grading a student and thereby determining his ability to succeed in the future. Moreover, the teacher of young or dependent students has even more power because the student needs and/or desires a great deal of direction and acceptance by the teacher. Thus the teacher is in a very good position to persuade, and possibly demand, that students behave in the desired manner.

The students' acceptance of the teacher's persuasive attempts and demands is related to their respect for and perceived dependence on the teacher. If the students feel that their teacher is not deserving of respect and obedience, they will not be moved by his attempt to influence them or his use of informal rewards and punishments. This type of resistance might lead the teacher to resort to the least effective means of influence at his disposal—namely, coercion based upon withdrawal of rewards and imposition of punishments.

In the Thai situation, the Chinese students, like all students in Thailand, hold the teacher in extreme respect. However, the Chinese are even more susceptible to their teachers' influence because of their dependency and the disorientation caused by the desocialization pressures.

The effectiveness of a teacher's power (whether in Thailand or the United States) to bring about changes in student values and attitudes is clarified by Kelman's (1961) analysis of three types of social influence and their effects. A student may *comply*—i.e., not change his attitudes or values but merely outwardly behave in the acceptable manner in order to gain rewards or avoid punishment; or he may adopt the behavior because he wants to be close to or be like the teacher—i.e., he *identifies* with him; or he may adopt the desired behavior because he feels it is correct—i.e., he *internalizes* the new behavior. In the case of compliance, the student will perform the behavior only in the presence of the teacher; when he identifies with the teacher, the student will perform in the "acceptable" manner only if his desired relationship with the teacher is maintained; and when he internalizes the behavior, he performs it because it is part of his own values and attitudes.

If we apply Kelman's theory to the Thai attempts to resocialize Chinese students, we may see the teacher-student relationship as follows:

1) The teacher requires the Chinese student to behave as a Thai. The students probably have a good deal of trouble doing this, and probably only half believe they should, but they do follow their teachers' demands in order to gain their approval and avoid their disapproval. They *comply*.

2) As they begin to behave more and more in the Thai manner—as a result of the continuing desocialization pressures and the teacher's requests and expectations—they receive ever increasing rewards and approval. This probably results in the teacher's becoming an important source of affection and acceptance for them, both of which the students want very badly. In turn, this may lead the students to be attracted to the teacher, and therefore to *identify* with him. Since the teacher is acting in Thai manner, a student who identifies with him will be following a Thai model.

3) This identification, in turn, leads the student to act more and more like a Thai. As a result of continuously behaving as a Thai and experiencing himself as a Thai, the Chinese student begins to feel Thai and eventually to think of himself as Thai, i.e., to *internalize* the values and behaviors of his Thai models.

Summarizing at this point, we can state that the teachers in the Thai school have considerable power and use it to influence changes in the behavior of Chinese students. In doing this they seem to communicate a clear definition of the new desired role as a Thai and to become role models for the students. Not stated in the foregoing discussion is the fact that the Thai teachers do respect the intellectual ability of the Chinese students and, in fact, regard them as, on the average, brighter than Thai students.

If we compare, at this point, the discussion of the reactions of the teacher and the school to black youth in the United States and to Chinese youth in Thailand we are struck by a number of critical differences:

1) Often, American teachers react negatively to both the behavior and abilities of black youth. They are often not seriously concerned with changing the behavior or abilities of black youth. Thai teachers, for the most part, differentiate between the Chinese students' behavior and their intellectual development, and are concerned with radically changing the former while enhancing the latter.

2) The general negative attitude of many white American teachers to black youth precludes any possibility that the teachers may serve as role models. The racial differences also make such modeling difficult. In Thailand, the teachers' rewards to Thai-behaving Chinese students enhance the possibility of their becoming role models. Moreover, the racial similarities between the Chinese and Thai people do not impede such a possibility. The effects of these factors are that channels between Chinese students and Thai teachers are relatively open, while those between black students and white teachers are often closed.

3) In the United States the behaviors of black youth that would lead to their teachers' positive evaluation are unclear. In general, teachers are more interested in controlling and keeping students quiet than in providing standards to which they can aspire. In Thailand such behaviors are clear, well known, and bring the "successful" students increased rewards in their school and future.

These contrasting teacher-student relationships—in the teachers' expectations about student abilities and ultimate success in school, in the teachers' desire to change their students' behavior, in the ability of the teachers to serve as role models for the students, and in the clarity of desired role behavior of students—all lead to very different socialization or resocialization settings for the black youth in the United States and the Chinese youth in Thailand.

In Thailand forces other than the teacher are also operative in the resocialization process. The teacher, through the desocialization and resocialization pressures, does control, in a sense, the behavior of the Chinese students and does present desirable forms of behavior for them to follow. However, it is unlikely that these would be successful if the school atmosphere was not considered desirable by the students, if there were no clear changes in opportunities available within the school and Thai society, and if support was not forthcoming from the older Chinese students who act as important role models.

The Thai school observed most intensively had a warm atmosphere. The principal of the school described it as follows:

[The general policy of the school is to create a] home atmosphere and to make it the most happy place where our students can study and play together . . . Concerning Chinese students (who make up half the students at the school) . . . we try to make our school a day home for them.

As a result of this atmosphere, the students have a positive feeling towards their school. These school practices also tend to reduce some of the negative reactions the students might have to the desocialization pressures.

A second very important power which the school has is the ability to open up certain opportunities within the school itself, as well as within Thai society, to those students who have been resocialized or assimilated or who are acting in a Thai manner. Students are more likely to succeed in school and be admitted to college if they act in the desired manner. This is especially important to Chinese students. A university degree is the main mechanism by which they can move up in the occupational status hierarchy of Thailand. By graduating from the university they are assured of membership in the Thai educational elite and of a very desirable job. The students seem to be aware of this and it presumably affects their behavior. Also, the students' families are aware of this and are therefore not as negatively disposed toward the school activities as they might otherwise be. They recognize that while the school may be attempting to change the Chinese identity of their children, it is also providing them with desirable opportunities.

A third important factor is the personal interactions among students at the school. Since many of the secondary schools in Bangkok have a considerable number of Chinese and Thai students, the Chinese are able to interact freely with Thais. Since the Thai students behave in the manner considered desirable by the school and teachers, the Chinese students when interacting with the Thais do so on Thai terms rather than their own.

Another aspect of peer influence in the Thai secondary school is the presence of assimilated Chinese upperclassmen. All students in Thai secondary schools must take an exam in the tenth grade in order to qualify for admission to the eleventh and twelfth grades. Those Chinese students who have adopted Thai standards are more likely to be successful in school and to pass these tests. Therefore, the Chinese upperclassmen who serve as student role models for younger Chinese youth will more likely be those who have been assimilated.

These three school factors—warm school atmosphere, educational and occupational opportunities, and the presence of successful role models—are important sources of power in the attempts by the Thai schools to assimilate Chinese youth. At the same time it is the lack of each of these three factors that makes urban ghetto schools such poor learning experiences for low-income Negro youth. As we have seen, and shall amplify in the next chapter, the urban ghetto schools represent a generally hostile environment for black youth. Teachers have low expectations of them, the physical plant is often old and poorly equipped, and the school personnel are all too often prejudiced against them. Second, the urban ghetto schools offer little perceived and actual future educational or occupational advancement for their students; college enrollment is very difficult, and businesses often discriminate against black youth, thereby making a high school diploma less important. Third, there is a dearth of upperclassmen who can serve as successful role models.

In summary, we can abstract ten elements involved in the efforts of Thai schools to resocialize the Chinese students into becoming Thai and which might be said to be key elements for *any* effective resocialization setting:

1) *Desocialization*. The Chinese students are detached from Chinese culture, language, and tradition.

2) *Specific "dos and don'ts"*. The Thai teachers and schools clearly specify the desired behavior for Chinese and Thai students and reward such behavior while punishing noncomplying behaviors.

3) *Warm atmosphere*. Often the schools do present a concerned, warm school atmosphere.

4) *Language*. The language of the predominantly teenage students is developed to the point where it can be utilized for interaction with the desired role models.

5) *Social interaction*. There is considerable social interaction between the Chinese students and their Thai cohorts as well as with Thai teachers.

6) *Performance*. The students seem to understand the new requirements and many do fulfill them.

7) *Formalization of socializer's role*. The teacher's role is formalized both as a knowledge transmitter and as a role model for nonacademic behavior.

8) *Peers*. There are Chinese and Thai peers who are going through the school at the same time, and who therefore reinforce the resocialization pressures and provide supports for the students. There are successfully resocialized Chinese students who are upperclassmen and who serve as role models.

9) *Power.* The teachers seem to have the power to induce the desired performance as well as effective control over the students.

10) *Future rewards.* The school seems to provide considerable short-range rewards and Thai society seems to provide the opportunity for long-range rewards for Thais and assimilated Chinese, but not for unassimilated Chinese.

While similar studies on the presence and effects of these elements in the assimilation of immigrant youth in America are not available, it seems likely that foreign languages were not permitted in schools, there was probably almost no discussion of the homeland of the students' parents, desired new behaviors related to loyalty to the United States probably were precisely defined and required, teachers were quite powerful, the students were dependent on their teachers for knowledge about the desired "American" behaviors, there were successful older peers who had been resocialized, and the future rewards in school and in American society were probably recognized. What may have been lacking in many of the all-immigrant schools was the presence of nonimmigrant youth who could act as role models. Nevertheless, the pressure of first- and second-generation immigrant youth from many different lands may have had the effect of reducing loyalty to the old homeland even if it did not emphasize an American identity.

Some recent attempts by groups of Negroes to emphasize a black identity may also indicate similar processes at work. In the past, schools—whether predominantly white or all black—viewed their mission as that of integrating Negro youth into the dominant white society. This meant an emphasis on the values and behaviors of white America with focus on the positive aspects of "whiteness" and a corresponding neglect of the positive qualities of "blackness." A number of studies[15] (e.g., the Clarks' study of Negro children who rejected darker-skinned dolls representing themselves and desired the

---

15 See Clark and Clark (1947), Clark (1955), and Goodman (1964).

lighter-complexion "white" dolls) have shown the negative effects for Negro youth of such societal and school demands. The Black Muslims and the more recent black power groups have attempted to desocialize Negro youths from their identification with white America and to emphasize the beauty, history, and glory of Africa and Afro-Americans. Clinard (1966) discusses, in general, the attempts of the Black Muslims to do this:

This importance of changes in identity has been particularly stressed in the Black Muslim movement in the United States. Working largely in some of the most difficult lower-class Negro slums, this movement tries to develop a new image of the Negro. In their small mosques in neighborhood areas great stress is placed on their proud African heritage and the rejection of the appendages carried over from slavery. The new convert experiences a "rebirth" in self-image, in which he changes his name (the names of most Negroes are those of their slave owners), his religion (Christianity was imposed by slavery), his idea of his African homeland, his moral and cultural values, and his very purpose in life. Among Black Muslims pride in African means that new patterns of behavior must be practiced by the lower-class slum Negro if behavior and the new self-image are to be reconciled. A strict private and public morality is emphasized for the "new Negro"; crime, delinquency, drug addiction, and illegitimacy no longer fit this new self-image. Family roles are also redefined; a patriarchal system is substituted for a matriarchal. Family responsibility is expected of the men, who are also expected to live soberly and with dignity, be honest, work hard, and devote themselves to their families' welfare. Women are to be treated with dignity and respect, given protection and security. In turn, women should dress and behave circumspectly, they should learn modesty, and thrift, and the women's auxiliary often even learns how to set "a middle class table" worthy of the "new Negro."

Although derived from a sect based on religious conflict, this general approach is highly suggestive for slum work elsewhere. Interest among American slum Negroes in Africa and its achievements has been developed as a method of change by others than Black Muslims. . . . Efforts are directed at increasing pride in Africa, such ancient cultures as highly developed Ashanti Culture, the Benin bronzes, and the new independent African nations. This emphasis helps to overcome the stigma of former slavery and the void in ancestral pride that had existed.[16]

Such attempts by Negroes to be considered on equal terms as blacks and not as aspiring white people have resulted in demands that schools consider and teach the relevance of Afro-American culture and history and emphasize that a black identity is desirable for Negroes, and in demands for more black teachers and administrators who not only can make decisions relevant to Negro students, but who can serve as models for them.

In contrast, then, to the aims of the Thai school and the American school to assimilate immigrants and minority groups into the dominant culture, Negroes today are demanding that the school socialize their children into the minority black culture.

SOCIALIZATION OF STUDENTS IN COLLEGE

The college in American society is in general a developmental socialization institution for American students. It usually does not attempt radical change in the basic values or self-identities of the students, but rather builds upon prior value structures, emphasizing some at the cost of others. The presumed major role of the college has been to enable students to learn new skills, to gain more knowledge, and to prepare for competent functioning in chosen roles after college. However, colleges do, at times, attempt and/or create significant changes in student values as a result of the nature of the college or of particular types of students.

---

16   M. B. Clinard, *Slums and Community Development: Experiment in Self Help.* New York: The Free Press, 1966, p. 319. Copyright ©1966 by The MacMillan Company.

In a very extensive and excellent review of the literature on *Impact of College on Students* Feldman and Newcomb (1969) conclude that colleges *do* effect changes in students.

Most salient are increases in "open mindedness" (reflected by declining authoritarianism, dogmatism, and prejudice), decreasing conservatism in regard to public issues, and growing sensitivity to aesthetic and "inner" experiences. In addition a majority of studies show declining commitment to religion, increases in intellectual interests and capacities, and increases in independence, dominance, and confidence as well as in readiness to express impulses. [17]

The authors caution us about the extent of these changes and the exclusiveness of colleges as the source of impact. Similar trends also seem to be occurring in noncollege individuals of the same age. Nevertheless they do feel that "it seems altogether likely that some students in some colleges experience some changes that are *attributable* to the fact of being in college."

These changes are produced by a number of different influences within the college: the characteristics of students when they enter college, the effects of student peer groups, the effects of the interaction between the values and standards of student peer groups and the faculty, and the direct effects of faculty members. It is the last three to which we refer as socialization pressures in the college community and to which we now turn.

Student Peer Groups and Culture

The influence of student peer groups is related to the functions they perform in the life of the college student. Feldman and Newcomb in their review of the literature (1969) propose the following functions of student peer groups.

---

17   K. Feldman and T. M. Newcomb, *Impact of College on Students*. San Francisco: Jossey-Bass, 1969, p. 48. Quoted by permission of the publisher.

1) As part of the intermediate stage between the family and larger post-college world, the college peer group may help the individual student through the crisis of achieving independence from home.

2) The peer group offers general emotional support to the students; it fulfills needs not met by the curriculum, the classroom or the faculty.

3) The college peer group can provide for the student an occasion for and practice in getting along with people whose background, interests and orientations are different from his own.

4) Through value reinforcement the peer group can provide support for not changing. Yet, it can also challenge old values, provide intellectual stimulation and act as a sounding board for new points of view, present new information and new experiences to the student, help to clarify new self-definitions, suggest new career possibilities, and provide emotional support for students who are changing.

5) The peer group can offer an alternative source of gratification and of positive self-image, along with rewarding a variety of nonacademic interests, for students who are disappointed or not completely successful academically. Friends and social ties may also serve to discourage voluntary withdrawal from college for other than academic reasons.

6) College peer group relations can be significant to students in their post-college careers—not only because they provide general social training but also because of the development of personal ties that may reappear later in the career of the former student.[18]

People generally take into account or are strongly influenced by groups which they respect and admire (whether or not they are members) when they are forming or testing their own attitudes or behaviors, or when making judgments about an important

18   K. Feldman and T. M. Newcomb, *Impact of College on Students*. San Francisco: Jossey-Bass, 1969, pp. 236-237. Quoted by permission of the publisher.

issue. These groups are typically called "reference groups." This tendency is especially true for young college students who are going through an "identity crisis" (see Erikson, 1963), asking such painful questions as "Who am I?" "What do I want to be?" and the like. This type of personal crisis tends to make people much more prone to seek out confirmation for their values and beliefs from groups which they admire and those of which they are members.

Kemper (1968), building upon a considerable literature over the last two decades, has proposed that one can analyze reference groups in terms of three functions, the functions being performed by the same or different groups.

1) *Normative reference groups,* which the individual has to please either because of his membership in them and his acceptance of their norms or because of the groups' power over him. Each group (e.g., the family) provides him with "dos and don'ts" about how he should behave as well as certain punishments for nonconformity.

2) *Comparison reference groups,* which provide the individual with a frame of reference by which he can test out his attitudes, beliefs, etc., or learn new skills. Of importance here are role models which demonstrate for the individual how something is done, thereby providing him with skills which he lacks but desires.

3) *Audience reference groups,* to which the individual attributes certain values which he attempts to follow. The audience group may or may not take notice of the individual, but he nevertheless attempts to attract their attention and gain rewards from them as does an actor before an audience.

In short, the normative reference group prescribes what is right and wrong and is usually successful at the *attitudinal* level; the comparison-role model group provides the individual with the *behaviors* necessary to achieve the prescriptions of the normative group; and the audience group *motivates* the individual to behave in such a manner by providing rewards, or the expectation of rewards, for the desired behavior.

Reference groups may represent conflicting values and the same reference group may provide models of behavior the individual wishes to avoid as well as those he wishes to follow. The interplay of reference groups is one aspect of the socialization process in college.

An example of the operation of all three reference group functions can be seen in Newcomb's (1943) classic study of Bennington College, a very small liberal arts college for women. The general results of the study showed that the trend of change among the students was from a politically and economically conservative position to a nonconservative one. A nonconservative position upon entering college or the adoption of such was associated with prestige or status in the college community. The dominant norms and standards of the student body and the faculty were clearly of a nonconservative nature.

Thus the entering freshman who generally had conservative leanings was faced with rather clear choices; if she was to do the "desirable" thing, that which would gain her prestige and status, she had to adopt a nonconservative position. For the overwhelming majority of the students the values to be aspired to in the college and for which one was to be rewarded ("audience") were nonconservative. The groups of students with whom most of the girls interacted, and with whom they developed a shared set of expectations regarding each other's behavior, had norms which emphasized nonconservative values—the students were expected to conform to these norms and values ("normative"). Finally, the successful and influential junior and senior women at the college were those who expressed nonconservative views—that is, when a freshman student compared herself with important others (role models, friends) she was in effect comparing her initially conservative values with nonconservative ones ("comparison") and thereby learning what were the "correct" values.

However, the effects of generally accepted comparison (junior and senior role models) and audience (generally prestigeful and status values) groups can be seriously curtailed by a deviant, cohesive, normative reference group. In a study of Bennington College during the 1960's, about 25 years after the original study, Flacks (as reported in Newcomb, Koenig, Flacks, and Warwick, 1967) studied a small group of girls whose attitudes and values were clearly deviant from the dominant values of the college community.[19] He found that these girls were members of friendship groups composed of similarly deviant individuals on the campus, and therefore were less likely to change their initially conservative attitudes. Thus, it seems, the deviant group insulated its members from the comparison and audience pressures of the larger college community and substituted itself for these functions.

The socialization pressures at Bennington were probably more intense than at most colleges because of its small size and highly cohesive value structure. At larger schools one would expect more variability within the student body and faculty, and hence greater opportunity to join groups and to aspire to groups holding values more similar to one's initial values.

Influence of Friends and Friendship Groups

We now turn to the influence that friends in general have on a college student's attitudes and values. A considerable number of studies (Feldman and Newcomb, 1969) indicate that "When students do change, the direction is towards the actual or perceived value and attitude position held by their friends" (p. 243). This influence, however, is a function of the nature of the student's relationship—that is, whether the influencing person is a friend or merely an acquaintance. Wallace (1966) states that even though a student's potential friends are usually limited by dormitory assignments, students are differentially influenced by close friends and acquaintances. He found that nonfreshman *friends* of freshman students had an important

---

19   In the 1960's the dominant values were individualism and intellectuality rather than nonconservative political values.

influence on attitudes "which most directly bear upon the larger and often more burning problems of developing an orientation to life in general; problems of becoming an adult in an adult world. . . " (p. 114).

On the other hand, the orientation of the freshman students toward grades was associated with the attitudes and orientations of more distant friends and acquaintances, but not with those of their close friends.

Thus within the inner ("close friends") circle of a freshman's [interpersonal environment] the emphasis assigned to getting good grades . . .may not be an important influence dimension, simply because such problems may not be the most salient faced by freshmen considered not as college students but as persons in late adolescent stages of socialization. What might be far more relevant, especially in a freshman's friendship with older, more experienced non-freshmen, are attitudes toward life goals, parents, religion, sex, politics, etc. Outside this inner circle, however, the dimensions of influence may shift toward problems relevant to college freshmen as students, problems less complex, more immediately practical, and more specific to life in the temporary institutional context.[20]

While friends do have important influences on a student's attitudes, studies have shown that a student's friends tend to be selected on the basis of the actual and perceived similarity of attitudes, interests, and values. Newcomb (1961), in a study of students who were strangers and living under rather close and intimate conditions over a number of months, showed that the selection and reselection of friends during this period of time was related more to perceived *similarity* of attitudes and interests than any other factor. If this is true, how can we talk about friends influencing each other to *change?*

---

20   W. L. Wallace, *Student Culture: Social Structure and Continuity in a Liberal Arts College.* Chicago: Aldine, 1966, pp. 114-115. Quoted by permission of the publisher.

Newcomb proposes that this may occur as a result of a cycle of effects:

In the process of changing certain of his values and attitudes, a person may move away from certain old friends, and make certain new friends. But within new friendship groups, there may be normative influences (i.e., pressures towards conformity) that effect further value and attitude changes which may in turn cause additional reshifting of friends—and so on. At some point, perhaps, when a person's attitudes are relatively congruent with those of his new friends, this cycle probably stops or at least slows down.[21]

Thus similarity of certain attitudes and values plays an important role in the formation and maintenance of friendship groups and pressures towards conformity within these groups make these and other attitudes even more congruent.

To summarize, students change their attitudes, values, and interests as a result of the influence of reference groups to which they compare themselves, which provide them with information or skills to achieve their goals, and/or which pressure them to conform to group norms. They are also strongly influenced by friends with whom they share certain interests. Friendship groups also seem to share characteristics similar to reference groups, especially normative reference groups.

The Teacher as a Socializing Agent

As we have seen in our discussion of the teacher in Thai secondary schools, the teacher can have a major impact on his students. In college this socializing influence can take a number of different forms:

1) He can motivate students to engage in intellectual activities.

---

21   K. Feldman and T. M. Newcomb, *Impact of College on Students*. San Francisco: Jossey-Bass, 1969, p. 247. Quoted by permission of the publisher.

2) He can provide a student with feedback about his behavior and offer him critical comments about desirable ways of behaving.

3) He can be a model to whom the students look for styles of learning.

4) He can form close interpersonal relationships with students and encourage them to reexamine their attitudes or support their present attitudes, and so on.

Whatever form these influence attempts may take, in order to be effective they require many positive and meaningful contacts between the faculty members and their students. They also require some indication that the new values and attitudes will be rewarded both within the college, with peers and other faculty members, and after graduation.

A major stumbling block in the influence attempts by faculty members may be the lack of congruence between the intellectual and academic demands of the faculty and the pressures of the students' peer group. A large number of studies indicate that this lack of congruence does exist. However, Feldman and Newcomb (1969) caution us that taking a global view of "college as a whole may miss the large diversity of values and attitudes of different student peer groups." They point out that even in colleges which have strong student support for social events and vocational interests, there are academic and nonconformist subcultures which are committed to intellectual goals similar to those of the faculty. The major socializing effect of the faculty is mediated through the student peer groups. If the peer group values are congruent with those of the faculty members, then the effects of the faculty may be quite considerable.

The recent emphasis on student participation in colleges has reoriented, to some extent, the faculty and student cultures. Whereas in the past, student groups were involved mainly in social functions, many groups are now stating that what they want are more meaningful courses. The students are thus demanding more and better education as well as a relationship between intellectual and socio-emotional learning. Previously these were treated separately. The faculty response has been a confused one because while the students are demanding a higher quality of education it is at times different from the type of courses typically defined as academic. The resolution of this attempt by students (and some faculty members) to change college education must await future events. It does, however, offer the excitement of providing education which emphasizes the nonfractionated nature of the learning process.

One area in which faculty members may have a particularly strong socializing influence is that of occupational and career decisions. This may be true because faculty members are seen as legitimate sources of expertise.

While many or most colleges may have considerable numbers of student groups which maintain values incongruent with those of the faculty, there are colleges where most or all the student groups are strongly committed to values congruent with those of the faculty. In these cases the socializing influence of the faculty would be considerable. These colleges point out the importance of student self-selection as a basis for predisposing the students to faculty influence.

Additional factors which must be taken into account in such an analysis are the degree of consensus among the faculty on academic and intellectual goals (a lack of consensus decreases the influence because it may decrease the extent to which the students would be certain of future rewards), the extent to which extracurricular activities are congruent with the goals of the faculty, and, perhaps most critical of all, the meaningfulness of the contacts between students and teachers.

CONCLUSION

Typically, the literature on socialization deals with the development of an individual's personality. However, in this chapter we have emphasized the processes by which institutions try to change individuals through role pressures and the like. While doing this, we have presented two radically different approaches to changing youth. In the United States, school systems charged with the responsibility of helping lower-class Negro youth develop skills to succeed in the society seem to have failed. In Thailand, the schools reacted to the challenge of changing Chinese youth in an energetic and effective manner, a style apparently not very different from that employed in schools in New York and elsewhere when they were faced with educating and training immigrant youth.

One of the major reasons for the ineffectiveness of present-day ghetto schools, and their past effectiveness with certain immigrant youth, as well as the success of Thai schools, may be related to the students' social class or social-class-linked attributes and values. It may be that New York City schools were only successful in educating the middle-class-oriented immigrant youth. In Thailand, the Chinese, whether poor or middle-class, are *perceived* as having certain "desired" middle-class orientations; that is, they are very energetic, hard-working, and achievement oriented. They are also seen as intelligent. These attributes are congruent with those maintained by their teachers and are considered desirable by school officials. On the other hand, middle-class white and Negro teachers in American schools tend to *perceive* black students as being unmotivated and unintelligent.

The failure of inner city schools to respond to the needs of students has led to an enormous crisis; students and their parents, who were thought to be unmotivated, are demanding quality education and are willing to demonstrate these desires in a very aggressive manner. The school systems which have maintained an aloofness from the students and the community are now faced with demands to which they must respond and for which they and their staff are ill-equipped, both psychologically and in terms of skills. We shall spend most of the next chapter analyzing this school crisis and the attempts being made to change schools.

Up until the last few years, colleges have seen their major role as selecting students who could achieve at "desired" levels and then proceeding to provide them with the knowledge and skills that faculty members thought appropriate. Since the students were highly selected and were, for the most part, assured of achieving their occupational aspirations by getting a degree, colleges had few problems with "controlling" their students. However, major changes have occurred in the academic world. First, recent demands by minority groups, particularly blacks, for college admission have reduced the potential control over students through selection devices. Black students who are hostile to white institutions and mistrustful of white intellectuals are difficult to "put in their place." Second, many students are concerned not only with their future occupation, but also with their present living and working arrangements, which they see as relevant to both present and future. Hence these students are demanding participation in the decision-making processes at their colleges. This severely reduces the "control" by the faculty and administration.

These two major changes, among others, have seriously retarded the "normal" socialization pressures of the colleges which emphasized that the students were to be active in nonacademic pursuits but passive in their academic roles. For many students, friendship groups no longer are merely social groups but represent important intellectual and academic activities. At the same time, these students, both black and white, are mistrustful of faculty members and adults in general, thereby reducing the likelihood that faculty members will be seen as models. Exacerbating this entire situation is the lack of interest in teaching and students shown by many faculty members.

The result of these changes in colleges may be that the formidable socialization pressures that directed students' interests into social activities and future occupational aspirations will become focused on quality teaching and education. If this is true, we should look forward, over the next few years, to major changes in the institutional arrangements of our colleges and universities.

CHAPTER EIGHT

CHANGING SCHOOLS

The rapid changes occurring in American society have greatly affected the operation of our schools. The protest movements, the racial disturbances in our cities, the unionization of teachers, the organization of ghetto communities, the growing unemployment of ghetto residents—all these and many other events have brought into question the efficacy of the schools. There is a demand for a redefinition of goals and a reevaluation of the role of educational institutions from elementary through university levels. Any meaningful analysis of the schools' response to these multiple problems must consider the nature and function of the school as a total organization.

THE SCHOOL AS AN ORGANIZATION

Viewing the school as an organization involves examining the relationships among the different positions within the school. These role interrelations might be shown in an organizational chart, as in Fig. 3. This simple chart specifies that pupils are responsible to the teacher who in turn is responsible to the principal. In this formal organizational chart, no direct inter-

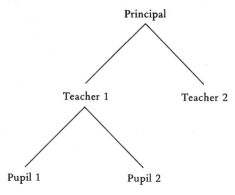

FIG. 3. Organization of a school.

relations among teachers or among pupils are specified. Obviously, informal relationships will exist among teachers and pupils which will influence the school's effectiveness. The formal organization is likely to be specified in a set of rules or regulations, whereas the informal organization will be supported by unwritten but strongly held expectations regarding role relationships. These expectations can emerge from four major sources in an organization: peers or colleagues, supervisors, subordinates, and an individual's own expectations about the actions he should take, on the basis of his own concepts, experiences, and personality style.

The effectiveness of expectations and rules in controlling organizational behavior is dependent upon both the capability of surveillance and the possibility of reward or punishment of behavior that is appropriate or inappropriate to a given role. The school as an organization differs from other organizations in these capabilities for one of its key roles—the teacher. In industrial firms the behavior of a subordinate is almost always visible to his supervisor on a day-to-day basis, if desired. This visibility is especially true for those role incumbents who perform the key "production" tasks. However, in schools, the role performance of the key "production" task is almost invisible. Miles (1967) comments as follows.

The basic role performance in the school—teaching—takes place out of sight of adult contact or supervision perhaps 90% of the time. Role performance is accordingly judged on formal, or once removed, criteria, such as the children's interest or the number of graduate courses taken by the teacher (regardless of content), rather than on direct observation and monitoring of performance. Thus, it is difficult to get feedback—to know whether a particular teaching behavior does encourage movement toward particular goals.[1]

This lack of visibility makes it extremely difficult to provide a system of rewards and punishments appropriate to the critical aspects of teaching.

Two other important aspects of an organization's internal structure are the extent to which there are different roles associated with the performance of different tasks, and the pattern of integration of these roles. In contrast to such large organizations as industrial firms or government agencies there is a relatively *low degree of division of labor* in schools. In elementary schools, particularly, the same teacher must teach many subjects[2] and perform numerous clerical duties, as well as functioning as part policeman and part counselor. The major basis for differentiation is grade level. At the high school level, the teachers' roles are differentiated on the basis of subject matter but not necessarily in terms of the other functions teachers are asked to perform—as clerk, policeman, and sometimes as counselor. Furthermore, teachers of different subject

---

1   M. Miles, Some properties of schools as social systems. In G. Watson (Ed.), *Change in School Systems*. Washington, D.C.: National Training Laboratories, NEA, 1967, p. 9. Quoted by permission of the publisher.

2   Experiments have been initiated to provide a greater division of labor along the lines of jobs requiring differentiated skills and knowledge. These approaches range from team teaching to differentiated staffing. This might mean that teachers specialize in such areas as curriculum development, teaching of reading, or computer-assisted-instruction.

matter do seem to perform their roles in a similar manner: ". . . the presence of a body of subject matter, an adult, and some children, tends to create role pressures toward 'explaining,' asking for recitation, and so on, independently of the personality of the particular incumbent in the teacher role." (Miles, 1967, p. 9.)

As roles are not very well differentiated in the school setting, they are also relatively *poorly integrated*. The teachers perform their similar roles in relative isolation from each other. Not only are teachers who are teaching the same subject matter not integrated with each other, but teachers at different levels perform their tasks without any sharing of knowledge, skills, or the like. Role integration is dependent largely upon the overall curriculum and the sequential properties of textbook series.

This is not to say that teachers are free agents. Rather, they are subjected to considerable, though not very visible nor well-coordinated, bureaucratic controls by their supervisors: for example,

. . . they are required to use specific textbooks on certain subjects and allotted a specific period of time to deal with the client (which reduces discretion). . . they are required to control the client by means of formal sanctions (which lessens the importance of expertise as a basis of authority over clients, and may conflict with the service orientation of teachers).[3]

The great difficulty with an organization in which key tasks are performed by individuals in roles that have low visibility, a lack of differentiation, and low integration (or low interdependency) of roles is that there is a lack of accountability for errors and incompetence. Since no one knows what is happening in the classroom, teacher competence may be determined on the basis

---

3   S. D. Sieber, Organizational influences on innovative roles. In T. L. Eidell and J. M. Kitchell (Eds.), *Knowledge Production and Utilization*. Eugene, Oregon: Center for the Advanced Study of Educational Administration, 1968, p. 134. Quoted by permission of the publisher.

of clerical and administrative duties or on the basis of pupil performance on standardized achievement tests. However, the accountability for the failure of students to perform adequately on schoolwide or systemwide examinations is difficult to pinpoint. This lack of accountability often leads teachers and administrators to charge that the real fault lies with the students, not the schools.

In addition to the internal structure of an organization, it is also necessary to examine its external relationships, or how this organization fits into the larger social structure. The American school is an institution of a local community usually subject to the authority of an elected local board and so is particularly vulnerable. Demands may be made upon the schools by influential community members and by parents who have heard about school operations from the sometimes distorted viewpoint of their children. In the past, schools were accustomed to the influence on policy by the community's "influential" members. However, more recently new pressures are being applied by the formerly least influential groups (low-income Negroes) in a style for which schools are unprepared. This has led to considerable turmoil in many schools.

PROBLEMS IN CHANGE

The structure of an organization modified by the characteristics of its particular personnel and the nature of their interactions are important factors in the organization's perception of a need for change, its willingness to experiment and try new modes of behavior, or its resistance to new ideas. Change may be dictated from above or it may be implemented through the active cooperation and involvement of all concerned. In the typical school organization both the lack of effective integration of roles and the low visibility make it possible for teachers to circumvent dictated change. Teachers relatively isolated from one another will tend not to share or seek out new teaching ideas. The low visibility of teachers makes it difficult for supervisors to introduce innovations or to assess the extent to which they are operative.

Another factor which makes change difficult is the anxiety teachers have about their status (Sieber, 1968). The gap between their desire to consider themselves as professionals and the reality that others often do not consider them as such may produce "status-insecurity" which makes teachers apprehensive about attempts to improve their performance.

Even expert consultants from outside the district are sometimes rejected because they threaten the teacher's insecure self-image as an "expert" in his domain. Teachers who are anxious to preserve the modicum of authority, expertise, and social standing that they possess, might reject administrative efforts despite the possibility of their better serving educational needs.[4]

This "status-insecurity" may also lead many teachers to reject colleagues who make innovative changes in classroom teaching methods (e.g., independent study for students) and to avoid informal communication with colleagues on matters of teaching and learning.

In order to highlight some of these relationships we shall present two studies which indicate the relationship between the innovative tendencies on the one hand and learned role behaviors, status-insecurity, low role visibility, and low role interdependence on the other. Carlson (1965) reports the effects of some of these factors on the introduction of teaching machines in a number of schools. In an attempt to realize the educational ideal of instruction for each student at his own pace ("individual instruction") teaching machines were introduced in a school. These machines were effective in enabling the students in the classroom to operate at their own pace. This caused a predicament for the teacher. While he desired to have all his

---

4   S. D. Sieber, Organizational influences on innovative roles. In T. L. Eidell and J. M. Kitchell (Eds.), *Knowledge Production and Utilization.* Eugene, Oregon: Center for the Advanced Study of Educational Administration, 1968, p. 129. Quoted by permission of the publisher.

students learn as quickly as possible he also had a conception of his role as a teacher. This meant that he had to get up in front of the class and "perform," that is "to capture and hold the attention of a number of students and to serve continuously as the mediator between the student and the information."

In order to fulfill this role conception the teachers made the following adjustments in their students' use of the teaching machine:

1) They gave slow learners "cultural enrichment" materials to make them move at a faster rate.

2) They allowed slow learners (but not fast learners) to take the teaching machine home with them, thus effectively "correcting" the range of progress of students produced by the program.

3) They extended the period of time over which the programs were used in order to provide time for group instruction and for interaction with the students.

The introduction of teaching machines also complicated the supervision of teachers. Traditionally, supervision of teachers consisted of occasionally observing the presentation of lessons and disciplinary techniques and studying submitted lesson plans. These were found to be unsatisfactory for evaluating a programmed learning situation, in which each student is working alone. As a result, principals resorted to evaluation by asking the students how the teacher was doing, by checking merely whether the teacher stored materials in an orderly fashion and kept machines repaired, or, as often occurred, gave up all attempts at supervision.

This experience with teaching machines points out a number of factors which social scientists have conceptualized as important for the adoption of innovations. First, it shows the rather obvious point that the human cost of the innovation itself is a critical factor. The teachers who had to change their behaviors and their perception of their roles in order to utilize effectively the new machines found the cost of such changes more than they desired to pay; their training, their experience, and their aspirations made such changes prohibitive. A related problem is the threat to the teachers' images of themselves. Miles (1964) writes that ". . . other things being equal, innovations which are perceived as threats to existing practice, rather than mere additions to it, are less likely of acceptance." This threat takes on added importance in the light of our previous discussion on status-security.

Second, the introduction of an innovation may change role relationships. In this case, it affected the relationship not only between student and teacher but also between the teacher and his supervisor.

Third, those studying the adoption of innovations have found that the less involvement individuals have in the decision-making process, the more resistance there will be to the implementation of the decision. In the case of teaching machines, the innovation was introduced at the administrative level and was created and developed by individuals outside the school. The teachers were not involved in the development of the machine nor, probably, were they involved in the decision to use it. Many subtle forms of resistance resulted. The effectiveness of this subtle subversion of teaching machines was strongly enhanced by the low visibility of the teacher's classroom behavior and his independence from others.

These factors represent only part of the problem of introducing or encouraging innovations in educational systems. Two other relevant factors, not clearly specified in the teaching machine example, are the teachers' feelings of involvement in the school as a whole, and the receptivity of administrators to experimentation.

Lippitt, Chesler, and their colleagues (1966) carried out a series of studies to assess the extent to which teachers themselves innovate and share their innovations with others, and the role of supervisors in inducing such innovation and change. The results of these studies indicate the importance of the involvement of teachers in their own peer groups and in the school decision-making process. They found the following.

1) When teachers feel powerless, isolated, and uninvolved, as is often the case, they are not likely to innovate or initiate change in their classroom or the school.

2) When teachers feel that their supervisors are not receptive to innovations, change, and risk-taking, they will not innovate in their own classrooms.

3) When teachers are able to meet in formal and informal meetings they are more likely to share their innovations and ideas about change.

4) When new teachers, fresh out of college, attempt to try out their recently learned new teaching practices and are blocked by the established group of older teachers in the school, they quickly lose their enthusiasm for introducing innovations.

In general, then, teachers tend to innovate and be more receptive to change when they feel involved and potent in the school organization.

Work in situations where one feels liked and respected by peers and supervisors is obviously more satisfying and fulfilling than work where one feels ignored; furthermore, it predisposes one to be positive and supportive to others. Thus, such a set up fosters a continuing cycle of change and support, invention and sharing of ideas.[5]

This research also strongly indicates that we cannot view the teacher as a separate entity in the innovation process. He is a part of an organization, and decisions about changes in his behavior are related to the other participants in the school setting.

Thus the adoption of an educational innovation is affected both by the nature of the school as an organization and by the

---

5   M. Chesler and R. Fox, Teacher peer relations and educational change, *NEA Journal* 56 (5), 25-26 (1967), p. 26. Quoted by permission of the publisher.

individual's own behavior pattern. Teachers, like all other role incumbents, will tend to resist changes in their accustomed role unless there are concomitant changes in the role expectations and regulations governing their behavior. This resistance is greatly facilitated by the low visibility of their role and their lack of interdependence with others. While teachers are members of an organization, the behaviors most critical for the implementation of a classroom innovation are not visible to others. Furthermore, the norm of independence held by teachers militates against a sharing of ideas that might be helpful in making them or others teach more effectively. Finally, the status-insecurity of teachers tends to make them very cautious in seeking out new methods or permitting others to be innovative. Teachers seem afraid to share their ideas with others for fear that they will not be seen as competent professionals by their colleagues.

The adoption of innovations may also be strongly influenced by outside forces. External pressures are not great in times of community harmony and peace, but when there is community strife related to educational issues or social change, the school may become a battleground. This vulnerability of the school has led administrators and teachers to be relatively cautious in making changes and active in their attempts to set up barriers to community intervention. Miles (1967) points out that as a result of this, chief school administrators have usually become passive and withdrawn from the demands of their environment. They feel that the school has little power to "initiate, develop, grow, push things, or be disagreeable to anyone or anything." They set up barriers to the community such as the ritualistic use of existing procedures, the continual justification of existing policies, and as much secrecy surrounding school issues as is possible.

Rather than cut themselves off from community involvement the school might work out a program for actively involving parents and community leaders in school operations to assist the school in adjusting to changing problems and needs of students, the community, and society.

HIGH SCHOOLS IN CONFLICT [6]

Both the need for change and the problems of implementing change in schools can be seen vividly in an examination of the crises currently facing many high schools. Student, teacher, and administrator are the chief protagonists in this drama.

The Student

The high school student, whether he be poor or well-to-do, is faced with a school environment in which he is a helpless recipient of orders. Teachers and administrators demand that he dress in a particular way, walk or talk "properly," and so on. A resulting sense of powerlessness is common among high school students. However, as one recent study of a few middle-class high schools indicates (Rhea, 1968), this sense of powerlessness may be subsumed under a faith in the goodness of the paternalistic teacher. The students in the schools studied by Rhea were not dissatisfied with their powerlessness because they were happy with the way power was being wielded by the school personnel who possessed it. The students thought highly of their superiors, especially their teachers. Rhea compares the student-teacher relationship in these schools with the patient's confidence in his doctor:

This is not only confidence in technical ability, it also includes the belief that the professional is working for the client's benefit. From the student's point of view, then, the teacher is both competent and benevolent, and the relationship is a professional one, or, as we have phrased it . . . a paternalistic one. [7]

---

6 Many of the ideas in this section have emerged from an action-research study being carried out by Mark Chesler, Alan Guskin, and Simon Wittes at the Center for Research on Utilization of Scientific Knowledge of the University of Michigan. We are attempting to help high schools deal with the conflict between the different groups involved in the educational process and to learn, with them, the nature of the variables involved in such situations. Research and documentary reports will be published in the future.

7 B. Rhea, Institutional paternalism in high schools. *Urban Review* 2 (4), 13-15 (1968), p. 15. Quoted by permission of the publisher.

This view of their teachers, however, is not always based on the teachers' performance, but is sometimes based on the students' *need* to see them as competent and benevolent. Thus students whose major focus seems to be getting good marks in order adequately to prepare themselves for the future view the source of these grades as good, whether or not the teachers warrant such praise.

While this positive valuation of teachers and schooling may be typical of present-day middle-class high school students, it does not seem to be an accurate portrayal of lower-income ghetto youth. The middle-class school is a steppingstone to college and a secure future; the schools attended by lower-income students do not provide such promise. Students are aware that the schools are not relevant to their futures. The school does not prepare them for the world of work; often they leave school, before or after graduation, unable to adequately read, write, or count. For many inner city youth the schools represent the frustrations they are to face in later life. Thus the myth or reality of the paternalistic relationship that Rhea states as the major factor for suppressing the students' feeling of powerlessness is, for the most part, nonexistent. The teachers do not give the students good grades, nor make them "ready" for college, nor provide them with the skills to compete successfully in the next level of education. Therefore the teachers, or school personnel in general, are not seen as competent and benevolent nor are students able to "will" them to be such. The myth or actuality of "institutional paternalism" does *not* intervene "between the perceived situation and the students' reaction to it, converting the situation from one conducive to alienation into one characterized by a high level of involvement" (Rhea, 1968, p. 14).

The result is that the students' sense of powerlessness and alienation becomes paramount in school. These feelings are further reinforced by the community in which they live: they see an extremely high degree of unemployment among adults; they see their parents hopelessly fighting just to feed their families; the parents often are the passive recipients of demeaning welfare payments; and the students see little hope of change.

These feelings of alienation are not new. What is new is that the events in the society have shown these students that there are ways to fight back. The students have seen that the civil rights protests have been effective in certain areas, also that riots and disturbance bring some immediate results. The tragedy is that these protests do not change the life of the ghetto residents. The students thus face the same terrible day-to-day miserable conditions but have learned new instruments for expressing their feelings.

In one school system the students openly expressed the relationship between the riots and their own protests. They told the superintendent that they were shocked that he did not realize that the urban riots were relevant to them. They felt that the superintendent should have realized that given the school and community conditions their own protests and "rioting" were inevitable. One student stated this very clearly when he said that the only way to make the school administrators listen to them was to cause trouble and riot. Thus the students see that protests may be effective in getting the authorities to listen to them, and use these as a release for the feeling of powerlessness.

In addition to perceiving the effectiveness of protests, the inadequacies of the school for their future, and their own feelings of alienation, the students have been sensitized to seeking change because the schools have become a focus for change in the societal discrimination against Negroes. Beginning with the Supreme Court decisions, in the years following 1954 there have been many pressures put on the schools to integrate and to provide equal opportunities for all people. More recently there has been a growing involvement of parents in the operations of the schools; they have begun to demand, through protests and the like, higher standards of education for their youth. Also, the advocates of "Black Power" have viewed the school as a major target of their protests for greater involvement of black people in the operations of community institutions and for a greater emphasis on the teaching of the positive role of black people in the history of the United States.

Thus the powerlessness of ghetto students has not been overridden by the positive aspects of high school education and the positive role of the teacher. Rather, the students have been sensitized to their lack of power and are beginning to use the forms of protest now common to American society in their attempt to gain a role for themselves in their own schools.

Moreover, the isolation of students from teachers and the growing lack of influence of teachers over students probably mean that we can expect increased conflict. Divisive social conflict is less likely to occur when a social system has many freely interacting and involved people representing different groups with competing interests. In schools, the clear differentiation of student and teacher and the lack of cross-group membership, involvement, or associations of a lasting character increases the probability of intergroup conflict (see Coser, 1956).

The reaction of the schools to the specter of actual and potential conflict has been confusion. Having depended for so long on the submissiveness of students, the teachers and administrators are not equipped to handle the students' demands. The result has been that in many cases student protests have led to the use of police to control the schools.

In summary, the schools are witnessing very rapid changes in the role in which students see themselves. Students are supposed to be quiet, passive, obedient, and so on. While many students no longer accept this role—for example, consider the severe student-initiated disturbances in high schools throughout the country—the expectations of teachers and administrators, as well as the school regulations regarding the role of students, clearly indicate that the other participants in the school organization still hold to it. This conflict in role expectations for the student is, quite obviously, very disruptive of school operations.

The Teachers

The teachers are also subjected to a lack of power in the operations of the schools. This, however, is changing through their membership in teachers' unions and their growing militancy. The growth of these unions results from a number of different factors: the growing need for teachers, the perceived effectiveness of protests and strikes in American society, the lack of school system response to the teachers' needs, and the vulnerability of teachers to school administrators and the community.

The need for teachers has placed them in a position where they can bargain and, if not satisfied, seek employment elsewhere. Related to this is the generally increased mobility of Americans. However, it seems unlikely that these factors alone would account for the rapid growth of unions. Similarly, if the examples of effective protests were not in evidence, it is unlikely that unions would have been viewed as a solution to teachers' problems. A teachers' union represents a role conflict situation for many teachers; they are torn between their role as a professional, which emphasizes freedom, promotion based on merit, and independence, and their role as union member, which emphasizes the fate of the group as a whole, seniority, and negotiation between union representatives and the administrators.

In reality, however, the teachers have little choice; they are powerless, their freedom and independence outside the classroom are probably more a myth than reality, and their vulnerability to other groups is extremely high. Becker (1953) points out that the teacher feels the need to maintain some distance or secrecy of actions from parents and the community because these elements are seen as uncontrollable. The unions have assured the teacher that he can maintain such control with or without the principal. They also provide teachers with a new source of power. Whereas teachers are often powerless in the face of administrative power, now they as a group potentially have the resources to resist such pressures, and in fact, force administrators to change. In the near future, teachers' unions will be concerned not only with wages but with school policy decisions, teacher training, and the like.

The feeling of powerlessness of many teachers does not mean that they have formed an alliance with the students. Rather, the teachers in the ghetto schools, where students are most sensitive to their powerlessness, have grown more and more distant from the students and have, in most cases, become more concerned with controlling their classes than teaching. In fact, in many cases it is the teachers who prevent students from having any meaningful voice in school activities.

An example of this is seen in Willower's (1969) observations of a large junior high school in a middle-sized city. He reports that pupil control problems were paramount in the teachers' relationship to other teachers, counselors, and administrators. Those teachers who were viewed as weak on control and discipline of students were accorded marginal status among their colleagues. One of the major problems of younger teachers was that of convincing their older colleagues that they were not soft. In public discussions and assemblies, teachers made special attempts to make sure that their students were orderly, often talking to students with more than usual toughness. In the faculty lounge, discussions among teachers were often dominated by boasts about the rigorous handling of discipline problems and by gossip about rebellious students.

There are many reasons besides the behavior of the students for the distance between teachers and students. A major one is teachers' fear of, and prejudice toward, their Negro and low-income students. Many of the teachers in schools with a large proportion of Negro low-income students are white and have great difficulty dealing with their own prejudiced attitudes. In some cases teachers have been reported to wash their hands after touching black students. Such teachers are unable to deal with integrated classrooms. Their own prejudice, or guilt about their ambivalent feelings, makes it difficult for them to teach classes of black and white students.

The teachers' feelings towards black students have been intensified by the rapidly changing composition of the inner city neighborhood and of the schools that service these communities. Schools that were once predominantly white have become overwhelmingly black, while most of the white teachers have remained. This has increased or activated the fears and the prejudices of some teachers. Another contributory factor has been the increased militancy of black people in general, their desire to gain power in their own communities, and their emphasis on black pride.

These feelings of threat and fear emerge from other sources as well: the teachers' traditional role as communicator of knowledge is being threatened by his need to control his class; the respect that he has assumed as a matter of course has been denied him by students who feel he is not teaching them anything; his methods of teaching have been said by many to be irrelevant to the needs of his students; and the rapid advances in all areas of knowledge have forced him to recognize his own ignorance or required him to return to school for retraining. Thus the teacher is threatened not only by racial tensions but also by anxieties resulting from ambiguities connected with his changing role.

Building upon our discussion of the basis of power in Chapter 5, the "institutional paternalism" of upper-middle-class schools and the tendency of teachers to control their students, we may be able to differentiate the general teaching styles of teachers in upper-middle-class schools and those in lower-class schools. In upper-middle-class schools Rhea (1968) reports the students' identification with their teachers and their belief that the teacher is really a "good guy" who looks after his students. Under such conditions the teacher is seen as an attractive source, probably as a kind of model, as well as being a technical expert. These feelings on the part of the students enable their teachers to utilize what French and Raven (1960) have called referent and expert power. Both these forms of power are based on a student's receptivity to the influence of the teacher; he wants to be close to or be like the teacher, or he believes the teacher is an expert and therefore right. As a result, he is prone to accept the teacher's influence attempts or communications to him with relatively little resistance.

Besides these two forms of power, the teacher also has at his disposal rewards and punishments. However, to the extent he can utilize referent and expert power he gains the good will of his students and enables them to feel that they want to learn; to the extent to which he uses rewards and punishments he is pushing or forcing the student to respond. When such force is used, students are more prone to resist. Although almost all high school teachers employ such forms of power, there is some evidence that teachers in schools with upper-middle-class students use less coercive, more student-determined forms of power (i.e., expert and referent power) than teachers in lower-class schools, who tend to use, almost exclusively, teacher-generated forms of power (i.e., rewards and punishments).

Administrators

All too frequently high school administrators are unable to deal with the increased tension in their schools. As the people who are the ultimate authority in the day-to-day operations of the school, they are responsible for resolving school disruption. Unfortunately, their training and prior experiences leave them unprepared to deal with the new roles of students as activists and of teachers as union members.

Following Jorgensen and Chesler (1968), the actions of administrators in periods of student-initiated demonstrations or disruption can be divided into four types of responses. First, whenever students are angry, demonstrating, or protesting, many administrators show a lack of willingness to understand why students are acting in this manner. They react to the student anger in terms of student rebelliousness rather than attempting to find out the content behind the students' reactions. This type of response usually escalates the student demands and reactions. Thus, when principals suspend student protesters for "cutting" class, the students react by increased demonstrations, usually with a larger number of students.

A second response of administrators when confronted by black student protesters is a denial of racial problems in the school. They state that there is no discrimination. Moreover, they continue, "There is no difference between Negroes and whites in the school community." They do this partly to "prove" that they are not racists. However, the result is that many principals at first refuse to consider any suggested changes in curriculum (e.g., black history) or dress (e.g., "Afro" or natural hair styles, or dashikis) which are based on racial or cultural distinctions, on the grounds that such recognition is undemocratic.

A third response, which usually follows fighting between groups of different races, is an overemphasis on racial problems. Whether consciously or otherwise, this response attempts to avoid any discussion of educational or school structural issues. Thus problems that may have emerged because of the students' feelings of powerlessness, the students' inability to relate to their teachers or counselors, and the students' reaction to the inadequacy of their education, become defined as racial issues. This enables school administrators to disclaim responsibility; they are supposed to be experts on intergenerational issues, not racial conflict, which is seen as a community, rather than a school, problem.

A fourth type of response involves a series of political strategies used by principals to avoid dealing with the issues presented by the students:

1) They maintain that there is a lack of focus of responsibility for rules—"It's not my fault, I have to take orders too."

2) They deny that the students' demands have a legitimate power base. They maintain that the demands have been proposed by a few students, thereby disregarding the substance of the demands and emphasizing the power-politic nature of the situation. In effect, the principals are redefining educational issues into political ones.

3) They maintain that the school policy the students want changed has the complete backing of the community, parents, and other administrators. Again, this says to the students that the principal has more political power than they do, and forces an educational situation into a political one.

4) They maintain that their age brings better judgment in moral and educational matters; therefore, students should listen to them. This type of paternalism, with the authority it assumes for the speaker and the ignorance of the audience, reinforces the negative feelings of the students for their school. It also tends to emphasize a power relationship.

None of these responses are relevant to the concerns of the students. Rather, they seem to escalate the conflict.

The tense relationships which exist between teachers, students, and administrators, as well as between the school and the community, are becoming more and more disruptive of the school, particularly the ghetto school. In a sharply increasing number of cases, the students—the one sector of the inner city school which has the least to lose, and therefore has the greatest flexibility—have begun to rebel against the treatment they're receiving. All too often their protest, whether violent or not, is immediately called "a racial riot." The community becomes frightened, primarily as the result of rumors spread by students to their parents, and the school personnel are unable to deal with the situation. The result, in a large number of cases, is that policemen are asked to enter the school and guard it.

In a sense, the entry of the police is the culmination of the control orientation of the school. With each successive incident the teachers and administrators use more and more coercive power. When students disobey the teacher, they are brought to a disciplinarian to be punished. When students try to use the student council as a means for being heard, they are told that the rightful place of students is in the classroom, and that they are too immature to participate in the decision-making process.

Students are criticized, punished, failed; they are thus left with few avenues in which to respond. They can submit to this use of force or they can rebel. In the past, most of the students passively put in their time. Lately students have been choosing another avenue open to them, that is, forcing the administrators and teachers to respond by the students' own use of power. This power to protest and strike is extremely effective, since teachers and schools must have students. The inability of school personnel to deal adequately with this power increases the effectiveness of the power because they tend to respond with extreme use of force; they intensify the students' feelings by calling in the police, suspending students, and the like.

Almost invariably the school personnel feel that the encounters are win-lose situations; either they win or the students win. The school personnel as a result of fear and anxiety exaggerate the demands of the students. For example, they often accept the rhetoric of "nonnegotiable" demands as true, and therefore do not attempt serious negotiations with the students. Because they have little contact with the students, they have very limited feedback with which to check their impressions. This results in the distortion of the message the students are attempting to communicate to them. Thus the high school students' desire for influence, to be listened to by the administrators, or to participate in school decision-making is interpreted as a desire for complete authority, and the students' desire for a better education is interpreted as a desire for controlling the behavior of the teachers in the classroom.

In summarizing the issues involved in high schools experiencing conflict and disruptions, four themes emerge:[8]

1) *The lack of student involvement in school decision-making*. As was emphasized in the previous discussions,

---

8   For a review of literature related to each of these themes, see Chesler and Franklin on "Interracial and Intergenerational Conflict in Secondary Schools" (1970).

students feel powerless in their schools and desire to change the present school structures in order to be more involved.

2) *Lack of social justice.* This is especially felt by black students. The lack of social justice is emphasized by the following issues: the small number of black faculty members and counselors; the absence of black and African history from the curriculum; a "track system" that often places black and lower-class white students in disadvantaged lower tracks; discrimination by individual teachers; and school regulations about hair and dress which discriminate against the new cultural mores of black students, e.g., Afro hair styles or dashikis.

3) *Low educational performance values held by teachers and administrators.* The students protest against the low educational performance of schools with predominantly lower-class students and feel that this results from, among other things, the low educational expectations of their teachers. Also, while teachers and administrators profess values of individualized instruction, autonomy, course selection for students, and independent thinking, they rarely make these operational in school settings. This is a grievance of middle-class students as well.

4) *Lack of fair treatment in student-teacher relationships.* While teachers complain about their students' lack of respect, students complain about their teachers' lack of courtesy and respect for them as individuals. This reciprocal disrespect and mistreatment is a vicious cycle which the students state they wish to end.

Redistribution of Power in the School

The present challenge to the schools calls for a redefinition of their function in society and changes in patterns of behavior involved in discharging this function. Changes in the structure of the school entail alterations in the roles of student, teacher, and administrator and in the pattern of their interrelationships.

Greater involvement of students and teachers in the decision-making processes is particularly important. This requires a major redistribution of power.

Power, which is desired to some degree and in some areas by both students and teachers, can be seen as consisting of two separate components: the ability to *influence* others and the *authority* that one has as a result of the rules and regulations of an organization. When students and teachers desire power they may want only to influence the decision-making process, but they may be *perceived* as wanting to take over the principal's authority. A redistribution of influence would permit students to have more influence in matters which concern them—discipline, student activities, and to some extent proposed curriculum changes, quality of teaching, etc. Student-principal committees might be concerned with some areas and joint student-teacher-principal committees might have decision-making powers in other areas. Students would be elected by their peers, to whom they report. To avoid choosing only the "correct" students no minimum grade-point average would be required for these positions.

Another more radical type of redistribution of power in the schools would be the *redistribution of authority*, whereby students would be given decision-making responsibility over some areas, teachers over others, and principals over still others. In such a situation the principal might be the equivalent of an executive secretary or chairman of an executive committee. An example of this might be as follows: the students through a student council would be given authority over student discipline, monitoring of the halls and lunch rooms, and student activities; the teachers through a teacher council would be given authority over curriculum, discipline of errant teachers, and assignment of teachers to specific classes; the principals and their assistants would be given authority over class schedules, relations with the superintendent and community, implementation of budget decisions made by an executive committee, and the general operations of the school not delegated to the students or teachers. The executive committee of the school would be made up of student, teacher, and administrator representatives as well as the principal, who would serve as chairman. This committee would primarily be responsible for developing the school budget and for hiring, promoting, transfering, and firing teachers. It would also serve as an appeal board for all decisions made by the student or teacher councils or by the principal.

What results would be expected from this student influence? First, the social psychological literature indicates that people who are involved in making decisions are much more likely to seek their implementation. This would mean, for example, that students, instead of resisting policies related to discipline or behavior in the halls and lunchroom, may actively seek to aid in the enforcement of such rules, assuming the rules are legitimate.

Second, students who have influence may feel that they are competent individuals who can affect their environment. Such students, particularly in the ghettos, may very well modify their orientation to their environment in such a way that they no longer see luck or chance as a major determinant of their lives, but rather that they can have influence over events.

Third, the students' feelings of competence and their actual influence may lead them to be more concerned with getting an education and pushing their teachers to give them such. With others expecting them to be competent or have influence, students may see themselves in this light. Their teachers may then tend to see them as more competent and influential because they are. The social psychological literature emphasizes that the expectations of important others have a great deal of influence on an individual's perception of himself.

Fourth, the insight that students and principal gain into the behavior of each other may bring greater understanding of the other's role and more response to the other's desires. This may lead to less tension within the school and a greater tendency to take risks and be innovative on the part of the students, the principal, and the teachers. We have seen that the lower the tension in interpersonal relationships, the more accurate the perceptions of others and the greater the mutual trust.

Fifth, the more empathy and trust that one has for another, the greater the likelihood that the participants in the relationship will seek to enhance not only their own rewards but also those of others. Thus, instead of all relationships being marked by "win-lose" interactions there may be a greater tendency to compromise and negotiate with others.

Finally, the greater the cooperation between the different sections of the school (the students, teachers, and administrators), the greater the likelihood that the relationship between the school and community will be marked by similar cooperative actions. Since most information (and especially rumors) about the internal operations of the school that is available to the community is derived from the teachers and students, intraschool cooperation may lead to more positive interactions between the school and the community.

An increase in teacher influence may produce similar results. The teachers may feel more competent, may be more innovative, because of the more cooperative school atmosphere, and may tend to share their ideas with fellow teachers and thereby increase the overall competence of most teachers. These changes may also lead to better teaching methods, to an increase in instructional materials which are relevant to students' needs and aspirations and, in the long run, to better prepared and educated students. Moreover, the discipline problems of teachers and students may sharply decrease.

The redistribution of power, whether as influence or authority, within a school system is not an easy task. It cannot be effectively instituted merely by having the principal order it to be so. The problems and tensions present in school systems will not permit this to occur. Mistrust, distorted perception, role conflict and unclarity, anxiety, feelings of inadequacy and impotence, bureaucratic controls, and so on, will not end overnight just by administrative fiat. Successful restructuring of schools involves dealing with each of these problems, and many more, while attempting to achieve broad changes.

The techniques that can be used to deal effectively with these factors have been commonly treated as sufficient unto themselves. Thus training teachers to be more interpersonally sensitive through human-relations training has been used to change the behavior of teachers in the hope that this will produce more creative teachers. However, unless other changes are made in the school structure such training will not be effective because the role of the teacher and the rewards for his behavior will not have been altered. But if these training techniques are used within the context of a restructuring of the school as a whole, they may be very effective and make the restructuring successful. Therefore, training teachers to be more sensitive as they are given more influence, and giving students more influence and understanding of teachers while reducing bureaucratic controls may, together, prove to be very effective.

The specific problems related to the teacher, student, and administrator that might be in need of change, if restructuring is to be effective, include the following:

Teachers

1. Knowledge about students.
2. Developing teachers' sensitivity to their own feelings toward low-income and black students.
3. New teaching skills to make the classroom more relevant to students' needs.
4. General interpersonal sensitivity for working with others.
5. Skills in sharing problems and innovations with other teachers.
6. Skills in negotiating with administrators and students.
7. Effective strategies for using influence in organizations, particularly schools.

Students

1. Knowledge about teachers and school.
2. Skills in discussion.
3. Skills in reading and learning.
4. General interpersonal sensitivity.
5. Learning how to work with other students.
6. Skills in negotiating with administrators and teachers.
7. Effective strategies for using influence in organizations, particularly schools.

Administrators

1. Knowledge about students and teachers.
2. Sensitivity to needs of students and teachers.
3. General interpersonal sensitivity.
4. Skills in creating an organization sensitive to the influence and needs of its members rather than one based on rigid rules.
5. Skills in being able to accept influence from individuals and groups who are typically conceived of as subordinate in the organizational hierarchy.
6. Skills in negotiating with students and teachers.
7. Skills in effectively communicating with a school board and the community in general, such that both groups have adequate knowledge about the school, are receptive to the school's goals and changes, and are able creatively to influence school decision-making.

An additional problem which is part of the change process and which must be considered throughout any attempt at restructuring is the ability of the participants to work in an atmosphere of uncertainty. The transition to a new school structure will produce great strains and individual pain. Each sector of the school must be able to see the desired future—the restructured school—and how the specific changes of the transition period relate to this goal.

Techniques for Inducing Change

Chesler (1970) and Miles (1965) delineate a number of techniques which can be used to deal with problems just outlined.[9]

1. *Books and other material.* Books and other material, such as audiovisual aids, have been traditionally used to increase an individual's knowledge and skills about people. These rather traditional means, however, have often been unsuccessful because they rarely involve the reader in the process of understanding. Rather, they seem to be abstractions of experience which provide examples not very relevant to the individual's needs or experience. They may serve as important resources to other change techniques but cannot stand on their own. Chesler (1970) describes one attempt to use a mixed-media package (Lippitt, 1968) to enable teachers and others to gain greater insight into the problems of youth.

The entire cluster of units containing recorded and printed materials which focus on the problems of youth are designed to stimulate discussion around critical questions, to disseminate innovative practitioners' efforts, and to present findings, theories, and practices. The units also provide skill training exercises designed to enable teachers and discussion leaders who are listening and watching to personally adapt the materials to their particular situation and concerns (Chesler 1970, p. 17).

The use of such packages may be an important aid in giving teachers and administrators insight into the problems of their students. However, by themselves they still are limited. The

---

9   The reader who is interested in pursuing these and other techniques—their problems, failures, successes, and other related issues—should look at almost any issue of the *Journal of Applied Behavioral Science* published by the NTL Institute for Applied Behavioral Science.

teachers and administrators can still view these problems in an abstract manner. They may see the problems discussed as typical of other students but not their own; after all, they may say, they see their students every day and know that they are different.

2. *Survey feedback.* Another technique that has been used is the collection of data, by questionnaires or interviews administered by external researchers, about closely related members of the organization and feeding the results and interpretations back to the individuals being trained. This would enable teachers to see how their *own* students actually feel about them, the classroom, the school, and learning in general. The application of this social psychological method provides the teacher with information he cannot easily explain away, unless he criticizes the accuracy of the methods used. It confronts him with what his students think and thereby enables him to gain greater knowledge and, hopefully, insight into his students' needs. Miles (1965) has described this technique as it is applied in the industrial setting, where a work group may study itself through the use of objective data and make plans for change.

The aim is to free communication, leading to goal clarification and problem-solving work. The relative objectification involved in looking at data helps to reduce feelings of being misunderstood and isolated, and makes problems more susceptible to solution, rather than retaining them as a focus for blaming, scape-goating, griping and so on. [10]

This method has been used by a few social psychologists in educational settings (Chesler and Flanders, 1967).

3. *Sensitivity training.* In the last few years a large number of people have received training in interpersonal sensitivity through techniques utilizing unstructured groups. For the most

---

10   M. Miles, Planned change and organizational health: figure and ground. In R. Carlson et al. (Eds.), *Change Processes in the Public School.* Eugene, Oregon: Center for the Advanced Study of Educational Administration, 1965, p. 28. Quoted by permission of the publisher.

part these groups focus on the participants' giving and receiving feedback about their behavior toward others. They examine how the individual's behavior can be altered to make it more responsive to his own needs and those of others. These groups typically gather several individuals from different organizational settings in a relatively isolated situation in which there are few or no overt group rules for behavior. Thus individuals who are usually subjected to role requirements, hierarchical structures, and the like are, in these groups, faced with a completely unstructured environment. Uncertainty and ambiguity are extremely high.

The results of these experiences are generally thought to produce, in many people, interpersonal sensitivity during and immediately following the experience and, in some people, marked behavioral changes. There is some question as to how lasting these effects are. The problem is that those factors which make sensitivity training groups very powerful—the release from role requirements, the reduction of anchorages for attitudes and beliefs, the unstructured situation—quickly disappear when the individual returns to his organization. In its place the old requirements, people, and roles reappear. As a result, the individual may return to the old behavior pattern or leave the organization.

For this reason, the practitioners of this technique have increased the scope of these groups. First, they have, when attempting organizational changes, tried to bring together organizational "families" in the same group; that is, they have taken all the people in top management positions from one organization, or all the individuals in a section, and trained them together. Thus when these people return to their organization there is wide support for the new behaviors and the subsequent changes based on them.

Second, in order to enable individuals or organizational "families" to have the ability to implement their new behaviors or techniques, the practitioners have added new, more structured techniques, such as role playing and skill practice exercises. Chesler (1970) describes these as follows.

Under the protection of playing out an "artificial" drama, players can take risks in exposing themselves or experimenting with new behaviors that would ordinarily be quite threatening. When these experiences are discussed later, efforts can be made to transfer learning from this dramatic representation of life to actual situations. Skill practice exercises also utilize a deliberately structured situation and a norm of experimentation to support the learning and trying out of new behaviors. Practices in the interpersonal skills of giving and receiving feedback, of value clarification, of conflict resolution, and of listening intently to others' messages are examples relevant to improved teaching (or administration).[11]

The technique of sensitivity training as enhanced by the use of the organizational families, skill practices, and role playing are useful tools for reinforcing and initiating a restructuring of the school as an organization. By itself it will sensitize people to their own needs and those of others; combined with school reorganization it may be instrumental in developing the changes needed in our present educational system.

4. *Confrontation.* While sensitivity training tends to start with an emphasis on the individuals involved in the group rather than factors external to the group, a confrontation approach involves the presentation of an externally imposed dilemma or serious problem which the participants must resolve. This presentation is usually quite real for the members present. The participants are given a wide range of resource materials which are potentially appropriate for an investigation and/or resolution of the confrontation.

One type of confrontation training session would require the participants to negotiate with each other in order to reach a satisfactory resolution to their mutual problem. For example, the members of a training group might be divided into subgroups which have to compete to build the highest and most

---

11 M. Chesler, Teacher training designs for improving instruction in interracial classrooms. Unpublished manuscript. CRUSK, ISR, University of Michigan, Ann Arbor, 1970.

beautiful tower. They are told that all the material they can use to make the tower is on a center table, but that the only way they can get any of it is for every subgroup to agree that the requesting subgroup can have it. In other words, they must negotiate to reach their goal. The members thus begin to learn the difficult art of negotiation. The tower-building session is followed by intensive discussions about the negotiation process just completed.

5. *Simulation.* A slightly different approach has been presented by social scientists interested in the simulation or gaming approach to training. In this type of training the participants are given roles to perform and are faced with "real life" problems. As a result of having to resolve these problems in a "laboratory" setting the participants are able to see how they behave as well as experiment with new types of behaviors. This method has also been used for instructional purposes in high schools (see Chapter 3). For example, the participants are asked to play the role of heads of countries faced with a major problem. Their responsibility is to resolve the problem between their countries without starting a war.

Applying this approach to the restructuring of a school, the students, teachers, and administrative staff might first play their own everyday roles in facing a threatened school boycott by students or teachers. This could be followed with teachers playing the role of students, administrators acting as teachers, and students as administrators, and so on. After each of these simulation events the participants would discuss their feelings and why they made particular kinds of decisions. The results of such exercises might be greater empathy with the problems of others as well as a smoother transition from the traditional hierarchical bureaucratic school structure to a more diffuse restructured one.

CONCLUSION

In this chapter we have tried to show how social psychologists are attempting to apply their knowledge and skills to understanding and changing schools experiencing conflict. In order to place these efforts in the context of a school as an organization we reviewed a number of key organizational variables that have been used to analyze the social structure of schools.

The discussion of the school as an organization emphasized the importance of understanding the nature of different roles in the school, and some of the difficulties involved in changing them. This was followed by a discussion of the relative invisibility of the key performance role in a school—the teacher—and of his lack of interdependence with other role performers (division of labor), the poor integration of roles, the vulnerability of schools to community pressure, and the status insecurity of teachers.

These organizational variables were then related to resistance to the adoption of innovations in schools. Resistance to such adoption was also discussed in terms of other variables: the teacher's sense of competence and need to perform, the effects of innovation on existing interrole relationships, the degree of involvement in school decisions including the adoption of innovations, and the receptivity of the administration to innovation.

Most of the chapter was devoted to an analysis of high schools in conflict. Emphasis in this analysis was placed on the role of students, teachers, and administrators in such schools and the strategies for changing schools in order to make them more responsive to the needs of students and of society in general. Four major themes common to most high schools experiencing conflict and disruption were highlighted: the lack of student involvement in school decision making, the lack of social justice, low educational performance values held by teachers and administrators, and the lack of fair treatment of each other by both teachers and students.

Two potential changes in school structure were discussed, one dealing with a redistribution of *influence* in the school so that teachers and students would have considerable influence in decisions, and one dealing with a redistribution of *authority* in the school so that teachers, students, and administrators would make decisions as separate groups as well as in collaboration with the other groups. These changes were discussed in the light of our earlier analysis of organizational structures. It was emphasized that in order for these changes to be realized, a number of important individual and interpersonal problems of teachers, students, and administrators would have to be resolved through training activities. These problems include knowledge about other participants in the school, sensitivity to other groups in the school, skills in teaching and discussing, skills in negotiation and working with others, and skills in utilizing influence within organizational settings. A number of different techniques for inducing these changes were discussed.

Although we have suggested techniques for facilitating change in the schools, many of the problems faced by the schools are created by the larger social, political, and economic order and many of them can only be resolved effectively and permanently at the level of governmental decision-making, e.g., by increasing funds provided to local school districts, decentralizing school systems, and banning school and housing segregation. The techniques for fostering such political changes are beyond the scope of this book.

Finally, while we have not discussed the application of the techniques discussed above to the changing of colleges, many or all of these approaches seem appropriate for such change attempts, though some of the major differences between the two types of institutions may require adjustment in the change efforts.

The next chapter is concerned with a case study of a relatively successful change attempt at one high school which highlighted many of the previously discussed techniques and problems.

CHAPTER NINE

CASE STUDY OF
A CHANGE ATTEMPT

We have discussed at some length the different techniques that social psychologists might use in helping schools to be more responsive to the needs of their students. In this case study we present a fairly successful attempt at such a change effort which utilized a number of these procedures. The high school at which the attempt took place has about 1300 students, of whom 9% are black, 12% are Mexican-American and the rest are "Anglos" (Caucasian Americans); all the teachers are "Anglos." The school is located in a city of about 30,000 people. The change effort at the school was carried out by an experienced applied social psychologist who was an outside consultant to the school. He was assisted by four youth consultants (two high school and two college students) whom he had previously trained in a different part of the state. The chief consultant had a good relationship with the school and principal prior to starting this project.[1]

---

[1]   This change effort was part of a larger action-research project which included seven schools spread throughout the United States. The project was funded by the Ford Foundation. The case study is adapted from a project report of all seven schools written by Mark Chesler, Jan Franklin, and Alan Guskin.

The major change attempt in the high school was a three-week workshop that took place during late June and early July. Forty high school students plus twelve teachers and the principal met during this time to work on school problems and issues. The student participants in this workshop were chosen by the principal and included ten black youngsters, an equivalent number of Mexican-American students, and twenty "Anglo" youngsters. The central purpose of this workshop was for students and teachers to develop some collaborative relationships whereby they might work together to improve school life. In addition, it was designed to help youngsters learn how to understand and how to articulate their own sense of concern with the school, and for them to learn how to organize grievances in ways that might be conducive to bringing about change.

The first several days of the workshop focused on efforts to diagnose school conditions. Part of the purpose of this diagnosis was to build a feeling of concern, and to create the necessary interpersonal relationships among workshop members that could support the later development of specific tactics for change. These activities were supported by the staff's efforts to help participants diagnose the sources of power, concern, and educational expertise in the school, and to help youngsters and adults overcome their apathy at being in a summer workshop program. Films were used as discussion provokers, including "That's Me," a pictorial story of urban Mexican-American families, and "A Chairy Tale," a pictorial representation of problems in superior-subordinate relationships and the mutually destructive character of oppression and dominance. Large group meetings were used as forums for the discussion of films and grievances, and small group meetings were utilized to generate diagnostic activities.

Subsequent attention was given to the development of skills in group organization, discussion leadership, and political management. Some of these skills included rather intellectual concerns, such as how to ask questions, how to help the teacher teach you, how to express interest in topics, how to help groups stay on certain topics. In addition, some interpersonal skills were focused on, such as how to engage another person in meaningful dialogue, and how persons in a group can give support to one another's movement on their own intellectual and personal growth. Finally, substantial time was spent on what may be called organizing or political skills; here central attention was given to the problems and tactics in organizing a group to do productive work and in organizing a mass of persons into interest groups that can take disciplined action on their concerns.

A third major focus of the workshop was the content of black experience, youth experience, and the nature of schools and school systems. Black experience was explored through the use of black consultants who talked about major organizing and expressive experiments in urban areas throughout the region, and in listening to and discussing the speeches of Malcolm X and other black leaders. The youth rebellion was also examined, in the context of the needs and concerns of young people in colleges and high schools of the state. Finally, the school experience was examined in terms of curriculum content, instructional organization, and school management. Students and teachers examined the specific character of the power structure of the community and the way that structure influenced certain decisions and options open to the school system.

One of the devices used to help students and teachers learn about the political character of the community was an exercise in "guerrilla theater." This tactic involved the simulation of a real problem, and attempted to have participants react to the issue without their being aware of the fact of simulation. In this specific instance, it was clear to the consultant and principal that the most difficult problem participants would have to deal with when they returned to school was the reaction of the local community to their being in a workshop concerned with student unrest. At the beginning of one day of the workshop the principal read a letter that he had allegedly received in the mail. It was from one of the leading conservative politicians in town, and it stated that this workshop was obviously nothing more than an exercise in brainwashing by outside consultants who were interested in foisting Communist tactics upon the student body and faculty. The letter went on to say that clearly the students and faculty members were not to blame; in fact, they were seen as the dupes of vicious and unethical consultants and organizers who were attempting to get students riled up to challenge good order and moral concern in the school. The consultant became quite visibly upset, presumably at the personally vilifying contents of the letter. Participants very quickly became angry at the writer and threatened to storm his house to force him to take back his threats. At this point the consultant and the principal told the group that the letter was a simulation and that no such charges actually had been made. They questioned the participants about the efficacy of their rage and the futility of storming downtown to the home of the alleged letter writer. At this point it became possible to talk realistically about means of confronting the power structure of the town and the level of reality of people's feelings about power. Gone was the comfort of abstract discussions of what one "ought to do" when faced with severe political odds.

Response to this "guerrilla theater" led to another major activity in the workshop. One day during each of the three weeks the public at large was invited to attend the workshop to see what was happening. Word of such public meetings was spread by mouth, by informal association, and by advertisements and notices in the local newspaper. The first week some 30 community members attended, the second week 60, and by the third week almost 200 came. These public sessions were run by the adult staff the first week, by the youth staff the second week, and the third week by the workshop participants themselves. The need to host the community and to tell them what was going on in the workshop forced certain participants to be open about the experiences they had and the commitments they were making. It also provided the community members with some opportunity to understand, in the midst of a process, what kinds of changes and reconsiderations might be in store for them and their school. For some of the high school participants, it was the first time their fathers and mothers had seen them excited about an educational process.

The typical schedule for a workshop day was to begin with a general session where all workshop participants talked about the day's schedule and shared reactions to the prior evening's informal activities. Then, groups of teachers and students met to discuss particular topics relevant for later change designs. Some of these topics were the following: seminars for teacher training and orientation, review of discipline policy, Negro history, human relations, and ethnic identity clubs. After lunch there was usually a short lecture, a movie, demonstrations, or other inputs by a guest lecturer or by one of the consultants. Following that presentation, small discussion groups would form to focus on some of the generic issues surrounding schools, communities, black revolution, youth revolution, etc., that had been a continuing part of the program. At the end of each afternoon, another general session was held where people got together to talk about what had happened during the day and to gain perspective on the following day. Although they were not officially scheduled, evening meetings quickly became the norm.

Throughout the development of these learning foci the workshop gradually began to take on the shape of a major emotional experience for all the participants. The youth staff, particularly energetic, began to hold unscheduled evening meetings for students. As the teachers became more and more involved in the content of the workshop, and in the content of dialogue among themselves and with students, they, too, began to attend extracurricular evening meetings and parties.

It is important to note that the staff of this workshop included teenagers who were college and high school students. Part of the purpose of including young people as staff members was to increase the staff's ability to reach students, especially noncollege-bound students. It was expected they might find it difficult to relate to the adult consultants; in addition, the adult consultants weren't sure they would feel free in relating to them. The entire staff set some time aside every day to work on the development of their own team work; this was seen as vital so that the staff could present an effective model of cross-generational collaboration which workshop participants might incorporate into their own situation.

The final workshop activity involved a field trip for the participants to another area of the state. The purpose of this trip was to demonstrate to the workshop participants the regional and even national character of the problems of school disruption and the relevancy of their own workshop training.

Subsequent to the workshop, the chief consultant made several other visits to the high school. By and large, the pattern of these visits involved meetings with volunteer groups of faculty members who wished to talk with him, and groups of young black and Mexican-American students who wanted continuing consultation on the way they could approach change in the high school.

Students and teachers who had been at the workshop attempted to work in their separate groups to share their insights and experiences with peers. The small group of teachers that had been at the workshop was not able to make much headway with their colleagues; gradually they became an elite group which lost contact with most of the other staff members in the school. These problems were not quite as severe among the student workshop participants and their peers, although much the same phenomenon was observable. Part of the reason for this was the strong way participants approached their peers with "help." The consultant reports that he was unprepared for this eventuality because he misjudged the degree of enthusiasm with which workshop participants went back into the school. As a result, participants' enthusiasm for continuing work with faculty peers seemed to far outstrip resources that were made available for thinking through and planning necessary follow-up activities. The various reports and discussions at faculty meetings and seminars simply did not decrease the alienation and distance between those teachers who had gone to the workshop and those who hadn't.

By the following spring, however, it had become apparent that other faculty members had begun to respond to the constant pressure from workshop participants and to continuing consultant visits and discussions with the faculty. The consultant reports that it wasn't until the spring that the entire faculty came to a meeting the principal set up for him. A good deal of the resistance seemed to have abated through the role and the style of the consultant. It is also clear that the school system itself invested in follow-up activities by attempting on its own to continue the intervention program during the spring.

Evidence of the effectiveness of the consultant's continuing discussions with students can be seen in the way student workshop participants now exercise their sense of responsibility for the school and schoolwide leadership. Self-policing and responsibility-taking activities by students who were in the workshop became an ongoing part of current school situations. The consultant reports this in the following manner:

The workshop kids see themselves as conflict-interveners when students are fighting. They take the initiative and walk into a situation in a way that is very beautiful. They don't walk in like I walk in to settle things. They walk in by standing around until they know what the situation is and then they say, "Let's do this." It is a participatory kind of involvement in leadership and not the heavy hand that most adults are acquainted with.

These students work with the administration. They contribute their own skills and talents to the presentation of grievances and the resolution of what they see as destructive forms of conflict.

The consultant operated during the year in a way that permitted student and faculty members who exercised leadership in the school to test their ideas and gain counsel with which to plan strategies. Continuing consultation also was provided to the largely white Human Relations Club, the black Ashanti Club, and the Mexican-American group of Chicanos. In these ethnically oriented organizations youngsters have explored their own historic roots as well as concerns for their ethnic brethren in school. Once again, the consultant operated as a repository of ideas, as a way of checking solutions, and as a link to bring specific helpful resources into the school when they were needed by any of these groups.

In an attempt to assess the effectiveness of the workshop and follow-up experiences, certain students and teachers in the school (both participants and nonparticipants) were asked a series of questions. Most of the sample of students and teachers reported that they were aware of the summer workshop. On the whole, reactions to it were positive from both participants and nonparticipants. The participants, however, were more specific in their comments. The only complaints were that the workshop did not reach enough people or confront certain issues clearly enough.

Most participants felt the workshop focused on black-white relations. One Mexican-American respondent indicated that he would have liked to see more attention given to the Mexican problem, but felt that the workshop was probably a big help to the blacks present, and that he had been "educated" by the experience.

The participants had a clear and fairly uniform picture of the workshop's major purpose. It was either mentioned directly by them in terms of increasing racial understanding and communications, or in broader terms of conflict intervention and general problem solving. Examples of their statements of purpose follow:

To bring about a better understanding of race structure and relationship and a closer coalition of different groups on campus.

To establish lines of communication between minority students, faculty, and community in an effort to air problems and work on possible solutions.

To obtain nationwide perspective on problems of conflict between groups to gain ideas on promoting ways to cope with the overall problem.

To try to find methods of preventing or at least directing conflict towards a positive result.

This clarity of purpose and the unity of participants' motivation probably are reasons why the workshop was able to function with so many people. Most participants felt it accomplished a great deal and left with good feelings regarding their part in the workshop and their future role in the school.

All of the respondents answered in the affirmative in response to the question, "Would you participate in such a workshop if you had it to do over again?" Most participants, interpreting this question as if it referred to a second workshop, indicated that it would further advance their growth. Others felt they had gained valuable insights into themselves and the race situation. Responses from those who indicated that they were black stated that they had gained new self-respect and "black pride" through the workshop.

There were several activities which were evaluated as being particularly useful. Workshop sessions to which community leaders came once a week were most often cited as worthwhile. Other highly rated activities included guest speakers, large group discussions, guest lectures, small task groups, relationships developed, interviews, and films.

In summary, the workshop seemed to be quite successful. The reasons for this can probably be found in the unity of purpose, varied and effective consultants, tight organization, variety of learning experiences, and a definite stress on putting plans into action. There was no indication of a lot of discussion and argument which left the participants floundering. They may not have found answers, but they did find direction as to how to attack the problems at the school.

Bringing these directions back to the school was another matter, however, and one which was accomplished with greatly varying degrees of success. As was previously noted, the faculty members in the workshop experienced considerable difficulty in communicating with their colleagues in the fall. The consultants apparently made no realistic provision to help teachers plan and carry out their reentry as faculty change-agents. As the principal reports:

Project teachers are, generally speaking, much more sensitive and aware of the needs of all kinds of kids and particularly minority group kids than the rest of the faculty. And our problem this year, since the summer institute, has been to extend that sensitivity to the staff as a whole. We had a terrible time doing that; it is very, very hard to do, we didn't realize how hard it was. We talked about it this summer and made plans to do it, but we were quite naive in our approach, and we are only now beginning to break down the barriers to some extent. What has happened to us is that we have had enough publicity and enough outside interest in what we are doing so that we have separated out [the workshop participants] into kind of an elite group, and we are kind of constantly talking to those people, and calling them into conferences, and letting them help us with other schools, so that they are kind of big wheels now. They are quite sophisticated but they have lost contact with their own staff members.

To a certain extent they have been rejected, especially the ones that have been kind of disgusted and impatient with their colleagues. We have had to figure out some ways to overcome that problem and have recently made some actions which I think have been quite helpful, and so I think that it is a little more open now than it was at the beginning of the year. The first two months of school we just bombed out with other teachers, but I think now we are beginning to make a comeback.

Despite these difficulties, a number of important changes have appeared in the school.

There is a lot of spillover in this whole thing that is very hard to evaluate. For example, there is some evidence that the Negro parents now are talking to their kids about what we are trying to accomplish at the school. For example, at the PTA meeting last night there were ten or twelve black parents there and they don't ever come to PTA meetings. They were there and they wrote some things to us that were very complimentary, suggesting that they understand that we are trying to do something about improving the lot of the black students on the campus.

There are some other things that happen sometimes as a result of what the kids learned. For example, a couple of days ago I had three teachers and two kids come into the office with a plan to work on a segment of the curriculum together. It is kind of hard to tell where the major stimulus is, is it the kids or is it the teachers? I guess I don't really care where it came from, except that I am glad that it is happening. That is why our kids should be used in the next [workshop] as consultants, as people who can say some things that teachers don't want to hear and that teachers can't say to each other. And this is what we have done in building on the experience of the [workshop] to put kids to work with teachers and vice versa.

There were numerous new events in the school that were seen as resulting from the workshop, as well as attitude changes and increased communication. Establishment of an all-black Ashanti Club was mentioned by more than half of the respondents as a major change in their school. Another indication that the workshop concentrated efforts on "black pride," as one respondent put it, was the establishment of a black history course. This, accompanied by other attempts to broaden the curriculum, was seen as a direct outcome of views expressed and alliances formed at the workshop. Other concrete changes were schoolwide. There was an effort to get students involved in school decision-making, to increase communication through faculty-student discussion groups, and to establish a human relations board. The human relations board was mentioned positively by quite a few respondents, and rather neutrally by others. It is not clear yet whether it is a meaningful organization.

The principal reports that the entire program opened the eyes of himself and his staff in the following ways.

We have discovered how completely irrelevant the curriculum is for a lot of kids; we are using the figure that up to 30% of our kids are untouched by the curriculum and I think that the [workshop] has made us aware of that. We just hadn't stopped to consider that this was a fact. I think that there are some other factors operating in that that caused us to begin to look and those had to do with racial things. The fact that we observed on our campus that the black students were not a part of the school, that they were kind of a fringe group, and the same thing is true of our Mexican-American students, so that the racial things became the opening wedge that allowed us to look at the larger problem as a relevance in the curriculum for all kinds of kids.

The [workshop] has been valuable to me, and has increased my sensitivity. It has caused me to be willing to stick my neck out. Maybe I would always be willing to stick my neck out, but I didn't know where to stick it, where it would do the most good . . . I can recognize now that I am sticking my neck out in [my own community] where there is risk. I get some feeling of satisfaction out of that because instead of being the white liberal that just talks we have some action programs going on that really rub some people the wrong way and stir up some controversy and cause misunderstandings and so forth which require additional dialogue, and I think that is a healthy situation.

Examples of new ways in which the principal is "sticking his neck out" are in the area of curriculum revision. Responses of the faculty members who mention this curriculum revision program are rather ambivalent; some feel that it "takes up too much free time," or that the "leadership is not strong enough." There were, however, positive comments from teachers who consider the project "necessary and profitable." In conjunction with this program, faculty members mentioned a program for additional training of teachers in the school; this in-service effort focuses on racial issues in the classroom. There also were a couple of activities mentioned which never got off the ground—a student discipline review committee and a student lounge—but these were in the minority.

Along with these concrete advances, several respondents mentioned attitude changes on the part of some students and faculty members. Some faculty members seem more interested in student concerns, and communications with the black students have opened up because of friendships established at the workshop and maintained thereafter. There was a very high percentage of both students and teachers who felt that the school relations had improved and that racial understanding was increased. Several also mentioned that the administration is more receptive.

Another more significant change has been the increased level of student activity, particularly on the part of the black students. Many students seem more active and more highly organized. The principal also reported positive feelings about the quality and degree of student activism. Students walked out of school in the fall and organized a disciplined protest against unchanged conditions. When the principal agreed to meet with them, students were able to select representatives to negotiate with them. The principal was very gratified by this organized political protest.

We really came out of that thing with some tremendous kids. Some are now very aware of the nature of the problem, are quite verbal about it, and are able to hold their own in an adult conversation. Aside from that there are also some positive things, for example, we are having some lines of communication now with our minority group students that we didn't have before. There is a great deal of comradery. In fact, I am being accused in some quarters of the community of spending more time with black students than I do with white students. And I think that that is kind of a healthy sign in a way because I suspect that the black students need more help than the white students or anybody else. Now with the Mexican-American students we are not making as much progress, partially because we are not putting as much effort into it. I think that the potential is there, we still could accomplish some things that we haven't accomplished yet, and it is just a matter of time. We just haven't put the time into it that it needs.

CONCLUSION

In our presentation of a social psychology of education, we have attempted to give some understanding of the interpersonal forces which lead to the maintenance of existing school practices and those that lead to disruption and/or change of practices. In this rapidly changing society we expect to continue to see major conflicts in the schools between forces towards stability and forces towards change. Yet we expect that the schools will appear very different in thirty years, that the source and content of the pressures and their mode of operation will be very different then.

Today, the critical conflicts seem to involve the evolution of power of three previously underorganized groups: students, teachers, and the black community. There is already evidence that these forces for change are competing with one another, that the immediate objectives of "teacher power," "student power," and "black power" may be incompatible. If we can generalize from the demonstrations and strikes in New York City in 1968, those in the black ghetto seem to believe the answer to their problems is local community control of the schools, whereas the teachers' unions strongly support centralized control in the large metropolitan areas. Not only are these forces for change often incompatible with one another, but in their assertion of power they arouse powerful counterforces. Thus in some communities, e.g., Boston in the 1960's, where black pressures were toward integration (rather than separate schools under black control), the white community organized to resist change by electing much more conservative school board members.

The effect of the open expression of conflicting demands would, at first glance, appear to be disruptive of the educational process and disturbing to the individual administrators, teachers, and pupils involved. We believe that these tensions are symptoms of the inadequacy of current schooling and are necessary for adaptation of the schools to contemporary needs. Often black parents and white teachers differ considerably in their expectations about the behavior of teachers and their black pupils. Teachers and pupils, also, compete for leadership in the classroom. The schools must develop procedures for coping with such problems. The nature and extent of future conflicts will depend heavily on how solutions to these problems are institutionalized.

If true racial integration in the schools and community is somehow instituted, the individual classroom and the teacher-pupil relationship will probably be the site for coping with conflicting values. If, on the other hand, racial separation becomes more strongly institutionalized through community control of the schools, the classroom will probably be the site where separate group values are reinforced and the conflict will be faced at the level of the adult communities confronting one another. Similarly, the conflicts arising out of student power may be channeled into legitimized encounters within the classroom or into negotiations between student organizations and school administration.

No matter what solutions are developed, there are likely to be changes in: (1) role demands placed on administrators, teachers, and pupils, (2) the perceptions held of one another by teachers and pupils, (3) the mode of instructional interaction between teacher and pupil, (4) the effectiveness and status of the teacher as a communicator and persuader, (5) leadership patterns in the classroom,(6) reactions to deviance in the classroom, (7) the kind of socialization occurring in school, and (8) the manner in which administrators, teachers, pupils, and parents respond to further conflict and change. We hope this volume has provided you with some conceptual tools appropriate to your future encounters with problems in schools.

BIBLIOGRAPHY

Adorno, T. W., E. Frenkel-Brunswik, D. Levinson, and R. N. Sanford,*The Authoritarian Personality*.New York: Harper,1950.

Anderson, R. C., Learning in discussions: A resume of the authoritarian-democratic studies. In W. W. Charters, Jr. and N. L. Gage (Eds.), *Readings in the Social Psychology of Education*. Boston: Allyn & Bacon, 1963, pp. 153-161.

Asch, S. E., Studies of independence and submission to group pressure. I. A minority of one against a unanimous majority. *Psychological Monographs* 70, (1956).

Atkinson, J. W., *An Introduction to Motivation*. New York: Van Nostrand, 1964.

Ausubel, D. P., *The Psychology of Meaningful Verbal Learning*. New York: Grune & Stratton, 1963.

Bales, R. F., Task roles and social roles in problem-solving groups. In E. Maccoby, T. M. Newcomb, and E. L. Hartley (Eds.), *Readings in Social Psychology* (3rd ed.). New York: Holt, Rinehart and Winston, 1958, pp. 437-446.

Bandura, A., Vicarious processes: A case of no-trial learning. In L. Berkowitz (Ed.), *Advances in Experimental Social Psychology*, Vol. 2. New York: Academic Press, 1965, pp. 1-55.

Becker, H., The teacher in the authority system of the public school. *Journal of Educational Psychology* **27**, 128-141 (1953).

Beez, W. V., Influence of biased psychological reports on teacher behavior and pupil performance. *Proceedings of the 76th APA Annual Convention.* Washington, D. C.: American Psychological Association, 1968, pp. 605-606.

Bell, R. R., Lower class Negro mothers' aspirations for their children. *Social Forces* **43**, 493-500 (1965).

Bellak, A. A., H. M. Kliebard, R. T. Hyman, and F. L. Smith, Jr., *The Language of the Classroom.* New York: Teachers College Press, 1966.

Berger, S. M., and W. W. Lambert, Stimulus-response theory in contemporary social psychology. In G. Lindzey and E. Aronson (Eds.), *The Handbook of Social Psychology* (2nd ed.), **Vol. 1.** Reading, Massachusetts: Addison-Wesley, 1968.

Biddle, B. J., H. A. Rosencranz, and F. F. Rankin, *Studies in the Role of the Public School Teacher,* **Vol. 2.** Columbia, Missouri: Social Psychology Laboratory, University of Missouri, 1964.

Biddle, B. J., and F. J. Thomas (Eds.), *Role Theory: Concepts and Research.* New York: Wiley, 1966.

Boocock, S. S., and J. S. Coleman, Games with simulated environments in learning. *Sociology of Education* **39**, 215-236 (1966).

Brim, G. O., Jr., Socialization through the life cycle. In G. O. Brim, Jr., and S. Wheeler, *Socialization after Childhood.* New York: Wiley, 1966.

Brown, R., *Social Psychology.* New York: The Free Press, 1965.

Bruner, J. S., *The Process of Education.* Cambridge, Mass: Harvard University Press, 1962.

Buckout, R., and S. Guskin, *A Psychophysiological Study of Persuasion.* Unpublished manuscript. Bloomington, Indiana University, 1968.

Carlson, R., *The Adoption of Innovations.* Eugene, Oregon: Center for the Advanced Study of Educational Administration, 1965.

Chesler, M., Teacher training designs for improving instruction in interracial classrooms. Unpublished manuscript. Center for Research on the Utilization of Scientific Knowledge, ISR, University of Michigan, Ann Arbor, 1970.

Chesler, M., and M. Flanders, Resistance to research and research utilization: The death and life of a feedback attempt. *Journal of Applied Behavioral Science* 3, 469-489 (1967).

Chesler, M., and R. Fox, Teacher peer relations and educational change. *NEA Journal* **56** (5), 25-26 (1967).

Chesler, M., and J. Franklin, *Interracial and Intergenerational Conflict in Secondary Schools*. Chicago: Quadrangle Press, 1970 (In Press).

Clark, K. B., *Prejudice and Your Child*. Boston: Beacon Press, 1955.

———, *Dark Ghetto: Dilemmas of Social Power*. New York: Harper & Row, 1965.

Clark, K. B., and M. P. Clark, Racial identification and preference in Negro children. In T. M. Newcomb and E. L. Hartley (Eds.), *Readings in Social Psychology*. New York: Holt, 1947, pp. 169-178.

Clausen, J. A., *Socialization and Society*. Boston: Little, Brown, 1968.

Clinard, M. B., *Slums and Community Development: Experiment in Self Help*. New York: The Free Press, 1966.

Cline, W. B., Interpersonal perception. In B. A. Maher (Ed.), *Progress in Experimental Personality Research*, **Vol. I**. New York: Academic Press, 1964, pp. 221-284.

Cloward, R. A., and L. E. Ohlin, *Delinquency and Opportunity: A Theory of Delinquent Gangs*. New York: The Free Press, 1960.

Cohen, A. R., *Attitude Change and Social Influence*. New York: Basic Books, 1964.

Coleman, J. S., The adolescent subculture and academic achievement. In W. W. Charters, Jr. and N. L. Gage (Eds.), *Readings in the Social Psychology of Education*. Boston: Allyn & Bacon, 1963.

_____, *Adolescents and the Schools*. New York: Basic Books, 1965.

Coleman, J. S., et al., *Equality of Educational Opportunity*. Washington, D. C.: U. S. Department of Health, Education and Welfare, Office of Education, 1966.

Coser, L. *Functions of Social Conflict*. Glencoe, Illinois: The Free Press, 1956.

Davis, R. B., *A Modern Mathematics Program as it Pertains to the Interrelationship of Mathematical Content, Teaching Methods, and Classroom Atmosphere* (The Madison Project). U. S. Office of Education Research Reports, 1963, 1965. ERIC: CRP-D-044, CRP-D-093; ED 003369, ED 003371.

Dentler, R. A., and K. Erikson, The functions of deviance in groups. *Social Problems* 7, 98-107 (1959).

Deutsch, M., The role of social class in language development and cognition. *American Journal of Orthopsychiatry* 35, 78-88 (1965).

Erikson, E., *Childhood and Society* (2nd ed.). New York: Norton, 1963.

Feldman, K., and T. M. Newcomb, *The Impact of College on Students*. San Francisco: Jossey-Bass, 1969.

Festinger, L., *A Theory of Cognitive Dissonance*. New York: Harper & Row, 1957.

Festinger, L., and J. M. Carlsmith, Cognitive consequences of forced compliance. *Journal of Abnormal and Social Psychology* 59, 177-181 (1959).

Fiedler, F. E., The contingency model: A theory of leadership effectiveness. In H. Proshansky and B. Seidenberg (Eds.), *Basic Studies in Social Psychology*. New York: Holt, Rinehart and Winston, 1965, pp. 538-551.

Flanders, N., Diagnosing and utilizing social structure in classroom learning. In N. B. Henry (Ed.), *The Dynamics of Instructional Groups: Sociopsychological Aspects of Teaching and Learning. The 59th Yearbook of the National Society for the Study of Education,* Part II. Chicago: University of Chicago Press, 1960.

French, J. R. P., Jr., and B. Raven, The bases of social power. In D. Cartwright and A. Zander (Eds.), *Group Dynamics: Research and Theory.* Evanston, Illinois: Row, Peterson, 1960, pp. 607-623.

Frenkel-Brunswik, E., Intolerance of ambiguity as an emotional and perceptual personality variable. *Journal of Personality* **18**, 108-143 (1949).

Gage, N. L., G. S. Leavitt, and G. C. Stone, Teachers' understandings of their pupils and pupils' ratings of their teachers. *Psychological Monographs* **69**, No. 21, (Whole No. 406) (1955).

Getzels, J., and E. Guba, The structure of roles and role conflict in the teaching situation. *Journal of Educational Sociology* **29**, 30-40 (1955).

Goffman, E., *Asylums: Essays on the Social Situation of Mental Patients and Other Inmates.* Chicago: Aldine, 1962.

_____, *Stigma: Notes on the Management of Spoiled Identity.* Englewood Cliffs, New Jersey: Prentice-Hall,1963.

Goodman, M. E., *Race Awareness in Young Children* (Rev. ed.), New York: Colliers, 1964.

Gordon, M., *Assimilation in American Life.* New York: Oxford University Press, 1964.

Gross, N., W. S. Mason, and A. W. McEachern, *Explorations in Role Analysis: Studies of the School Superintendency Role.* New York: Wiley, 1957.

Gurin, P., G. Gurin, R. Lao, and M. Beattie, Internal-external control in the motivational dynamics of Negro youth. *Journal of Social Issues* XXV (3), 29-53 (1969).

Guskin, A. E., *Changing Identity: The Assimilation of Chinese in Thailand.* Unpublished doctoral dissertation. Ann Arbor: University of Michigan, 1968.

Guskin, J. T., *The Effect of Negro Dialect on Teachers'*

Expectations of Students' Ability. Unpublished manuscript. Ann Arbor: University of Michigan, School of Education, 1968.

Guskin, S. L., The influence of labelling upon the perception of subnormality in mentally defective children. *American Journal of Mental Deficiency* **67**, 402-406 (1962).

Guskin, S. L., and H. H. Spicker, Educational research in mental retardation. In N. Ellis (Ed.), *International Review of Research in Mental Retardation,* **Vol. 3.** New York: Academic Press, 1968, pp. 217-278.

Guskin, S. L., and R. M. Taylor, Educational effects of a school tuberculin-testing program. *Journal of School Health* **38**, 219-226 (1968).

Haefner, D. P., Modifying health behavior by persuasive communication. In S. Guskin (Ed.), *Proceedings of Conference on Behavioral Aspects of Tuberculosis,* Nov. 5-6, 1964, Washington University, St. Louis, Mo. Washington, D. C.: U. S. Department of Health, Education and Welfare, Public Health Service, 1965.

Heider, F., *The Psychology of Interpersonal Relations.* New York: Wiley, 1958.

Henriott, R. E., and N. H. St. John, *Social Class and the Urban School.* New York: Wiley, 1966.

Hess, R., and V. Shipman, Early experiences and the socialization of cognitive needs in children. *Child Development* **36**, 869-886, (1965).

Hollander, E. P., Conformity, status, and idiosyncrasy credit. *Psychological Review* **65**, 117-127 (1958).

Hovland, C. I., Reconciling conflicting results derived from experimental and survey studies of attitude change. *American Psychologist* **14**, 8-17 (1959).

Hovland, C. I., I. Janis, and H. Kelley, *Communication and Persuasion.* New Haven: Yale University Press, 1953.

Hovland, C. I. and W. Weiss, The influence of source credibility on communication effectiveness. In H. Proshansky and B.

Seidenberg (Eds.), *Basic Studies in Social Psychology*. New York: Holt, Rinehart and Winston, 1965, pp. 175-185.

Janis, I. L., Personality correlates of susceptibility to persuasion. *Journal of Personality* 22, 504-518 (1954).

Janis, I. L., and S. Feshbach, Effects of fear-arousing communications. *Journal of Abnormal and Social Psychology* 48, 78-92 (1953).

Johnson, T. J., R. Feigenbaum and M. Weiby, Some determinants and consequences of the teacher's perceptions of causation. *Journal of Educational Psychology* 55, 237-246 (1964).

Jones, E. E., K. E. Davies and K. J. Gergen, Role playing variations and their information value for person perception. *Journal of Abnormal and Social Psychology* 63, 302-310 (1961).

Jorgenson, C., and M. Chesler, *Crisis Intervention in the Schools*. II. A report of a conference of school administrators, Ann Arbor, Center for Research on the Utilization of Scientific Knowledge, Sept. 8-10, 1968. Ann Arbor: University of Michigan, 1968.

Kagan, J., Impulsive and reflective children: Significance of conceptual tempo. In J. D. Krumboltz (Ed.), *Learning and the Educational Process*. Chicago: Rand McNally, 1965, pp. 133-161.

Katz, I., The socialization of academic motivation in minority group children. In D. Levine (Ed.), *Nebraska Symposium on Motivation*, 1967, XV, 133-191.

Katz, D., and R. Kahn, *The Social Psychology of Organizations*. New York: Wiley, 1966.

Keller, S., The social world of the urban slum child: Some early findings. *American Journal of Orthopsychiatry* 33, 823-831, (1963).

Kelley, H. H., The warm-cold variable in first impressions of persons. In H. Proshansky and B. Seidenberg (Eds.), *Basic Studies in Social Psychology*. New York: Holt, Rinehart and Winston, 1965, pp. 65-70.

Kelly, G. A., *The Psychology of Personal Constructs*. New York: Norton, 1955.

Kelman, H. C., Processes of opinion change. *Public Opinion Quarterly* 25, 57-78 (1961).

Kelman, H. C., and C. I. Hovland, Reinstatement of the communicator in delayed measurement of opinion change. *Journal of Abnormal and Social Psychology* 48, 327-335, (1953).

Kemper, T. D., Reference groups, socialization, and achievement. *American Sociological Review* 33 (1), 31-45 (1968).

Kounin, J. S., V. Gump, and J. J. Ryan III, Explorations in classroom management. In W. W. Charters, Jr., and N. L. Gage (Eds.), *Readings in the Social Psychology of Education*. Boston: Allyn & Bacon, 1963, pp. 190-195.

Linton, H. B., Dependence on external influence: Correlates in perception, attitudes, and judgment. *Journal of Abnormal and Social Psychology* 51, 502-507 (1955).

Lippitt, R., An experimental study of the effect of democratic and authoritarian group atmospheres. *University of Iowa Studies in Child Welfare,* **XVI**, No. 3. Iowa City: University of Iowa Press, 1940.

———, *The World of Troubled Youth,* Reading, Massachusetts: Addison-Wesley, 1968.

Lippitt, R., M. Chesler, *et al.,* The teacher as innovator, seeker, and sharer of new practices. In R. I. Miller (Ed.), *Perspectives on Educational Change*. New York: Appleton-Century-Crofts, 1966.

Lippitt, R., J. Watson, and B. Westley, *The Dynamics of Planned Change*. New York: Harcourt Brace, 1958.

Lippitt, R., and R. K. White, An experimental study of leadership and group life. In H. Proshansky and B. Seidenberg (Eds.), *Basic studies in social psychology*. New York: Holt, Rinehart and Winston, 1965, pp. 523-537.

Lippmann, W., *Public Opinion*. New York: Harcourt Brace, 1922.

McClelland, D. C., *The Achieving Society*. Princeton, New Jersey: Van Nostrand, 1961.

McClelland, D. C., J. W. Atkinson, R. A. Clark, and E. L. Lowell, *The Achievement Motive*. New York: Appleton, 1953.

McGuire, W. J., Inducing resistance to persuasion: Some contemporary approaches. In L. Berkowitz (Ed.), *Advances in Experimental Social Psychology*, Vol. 1. New York: Academic Press, 1964, pp. 191-229.

_____, The nature of attitudes and attitude change. In G. Lindzey and E. Aronson (Eds.), *Handbook of Social Psychology* (2nd Ed.), Vol. 3. Reading, Massachusetts: Addison-Wesley, 1969, pp. 136-314.

McKeachie, W. J., Research on teaching at the college and university level. In N. L. Gage (Ed.), *Handbook of Research on Teaching*. Chicago: Rand-McNally, 1963, pp. 1118-1172.

McLuhan, M., *Understanding Media: The Extensions of Man*. New York: McGraw-Hill, 1964.

Michael, D. N., *The Unprepared Society*. New York: Basic Books, 1968.

Miles, M., Innovation in education: Some generalizations. In M. Miles (Ed.), *Innovation in Education*. New York: Teachers College, Columbia University Bureau of Publications, 1964, pp. 631-662.

_____, Planned change and organizational health: Figure and ground. In R. Carlson *et al.* (Eds.), *Change Processes in the Public School*. Eugene, Oregon: Center for The Advanced Study of Educational Administration, 1965.

_____, Some properties of schools as social systems. In G. Watson (Ed.), *Change in School Systems*. Washington, D. C.: National Training Laboratories, NEA, 1967.

Neill, A. S., *Summerhill: A Radical Approach to Child Rearing*. New York: Hart, 1960.

Newcomb, T. M., *Personality and Social Change: Attitude Formation in a Student Community*. New York: Holt, 1943.

———, Autistic hostility and social reality. *Human Relations* **1**, 3-20 (1947).

———, *The Acquaintance Process*. New York: Holt, 1961.

Newcomb, T. M., K. Koenig, R. Flacks, and D. Warwick, *Persistence and Change: Bennington College and its Students after Twenty-five Years*. New York: Wiley, 1967.

Pettigrew, T. F., Personality and sociocultural factors in intergroup attitudes: A cross-national comparison. *Journal of Conflict Resolution* **2**, 29-42 (1958).

———, *A Profile of the Negro American*. Princeton, New Jersey: Van Nostrand, 1964.

Rhea, B., Institutional paternalism in high schools. *The Urban Review,* **2**, (4), 13-15 (1968).

Rogers, C., *Client-centered Therapy: Its Current Practice, Implications and Theory*. Boston: Houghton Mifflin, 1951.

Rosen, B. C., Socialization and achievement motivation. *American Sociological Review* **27**, 612-624 (1962).

Rosenthal, R., and L. Jacobson, *Pygmalion in the Classroom: Teacher Expectation and Pupils' Intellectual Development*. New York: Holt, Rinehart and Winston, 1968(a).

———, Teacher expectations for the disadvantaged. *Scientific American* **218** (4), 19-23 (1968)(b).

Ross, D., Relationship between dependency, intentional learning, and incidental learning in pre-school children. *Journal of Personality and Social Psychology* **4**, 374-381 (1966).

Schachter, S., Deviation, rejection, and communication. *Journal of Abnormal and Social Psychology* **46**, 190-207 (1951).

Secord, P. F., and C. W. Backman, *Social Psychology*. New York: McGraw-Hill, 1964.

Sieber, S. D., Organizational influences on innovative roles. In T. L. Eidell and J. M. Kitchell (Eds.), *Knowledge Production and Utilization*. Eugene, Oregon: Center for the Advanced Study of Educational Administration, 1968.

Skinner, B. F., *Science and Human Behavior*. New York: Macmillan, 1953.

Stinchcombe, A. L., *Rebellion in a High School.* Chicago: Quadrangle Books, 1964.

Strodtbeck, F. L., The hidden curriculum in the middle-class home. In J. D. Krumboltz (Ed.), *Learning and the Educational Process.* Chicago: Rand McNally, 1965, pp. 91-112.

Taft, R. A., and R. Johnston, The assimilation of adolescent Polish immigrants and parent-child interaction. *Merrill-Palmer Quarterly* **13** (2), 111-120 (1967).

Thelen, H. A., *Classroom Grouping for Teachability.* New York: Wiley, 1967.

Twyman, P., and B. J. Biddle, Role conflict for public school teachers. *Journal of Psychology* **55**, 183-198 (1963).

Veroff, J., S. Feld, and G. Gurin, Achievement motivation and religious background. *American Sociological Review* **27**, 205-217 (1962).

Wallace, W. L., *Student Culture: Social Structure and Continuity in a Liberal Arts College.* Chicago: Aldine, 1966.

White, R. K., and R. Lippitt, *Autocracy and Democracy: An Experimental Inquiry.* New York: Harper, 1960.

Willower, D., Schools as organizations: Some illustrated strategies for educational research and practice. *Journal of Educational Administration,* vii (2) (1969).

Winterbottom, M. R., The relation of need for achievement to learning experience in independence and mastery. In J. W. Atkinson (Ed.), *Motives in Fantasy, Action and Society.* Princeton, New Jersey: Van Nostrand, 1958, pp. 453-478.

Witkin, H. A., H. B. Lewis, M. Hertzman, K. Machover, P. B. Meissner, and S. Wapner, *Personality Through Perception.* New York: Harper, 1954.

Wright, B., *Physical Disability: A Psychological Approach.* New York: Harper & Row, 1960.

Zigler, E., and I. L. Child, Socialization. In G. Lindzey and E. Aronson (Eds.) *The Handbook of Social Psychology* (2nd ed.), vol. 3, Reading, Massachusetts: Addison-Wesley, 1969, pp. 450-589.

INDEX

and response to leaders, 78-80
  vs. role perspective, 1-3, 17, 18
  theory, common sense, 33-35
Persuader style, 62-63
Persuasibility, 60
Persuasion, 8, 50-64, 119
  emotional appeals, 51-53
  immunization against, 56-60
  one-sided *vs.* two-sided arguments,
    57, 58
Pettigrew, T. F., 32, 198
Physical handicap, reactions to, 88,
  89, 92-95
Police, role of teacher, 71
  in schools, 152, 158
Political change, 172
Political strategies, administrator,
  157
Position (*see* Role)
Power, black, 126, 151, 186
  feelings about, 176
  of leader, 78
  and leadership, 66-69
  legitimate, 69, 71
  of models, 48
  redistribution, in the school, 160-
    165
  sources, 68, 155, 156
  student, 7, 159, 186
  teacher, 7, 97, 119, 153, 155, 186
    and socialization, 125
  vs. student power, 66-68
  see also Control, Leadership
Powerlessness, sense of, student,
  149, 150, 151, 152, 157, 160
  teacher, 147, 153, 154
Precision teaching, 44, 45
Preconception, 29 (*see also* Stereotype)
Prejudice, 25, 31, 32, 111, 112, 154
Professionals, teachers as, 144, 149,
  153
Programmed instruction, 37, 38, 40,
  44

Projective techniques, 23
Proshansky, H., 192, 194, 195, 196
Protestant ethic, 112
Protests, student, 151, 152, 158, 185
Psychodynamic explanation of
  scapegoating, 85-87
Psychological reports, bias induced
  by, 12-15, 29
Punishment, teacher use of, 43, 45,
  51, 52, 62, 116
  and leadership, 69, 70, 71, 75
  see also Coercive power
Pupil (*see* Student)

Questions, use of, in instruction, 37,
  38, 83

Race, and attribution of responsi-
  bility, 34
Racial attitudes, 32
Racial differences, and credibility
  of teacher, 60, 68
  as deviance, 88
Racial integration, 187
Racial problems, 157
Racial stereotypes, 29, 30
Rankin, F. F., 190
Raven, B., 69, 155, 193
Reading, and conceptual tempo, 25
  and expository method, 42
  as verbal interaction, 37
Rebelliousness, student, 89-91, 156,
  175
  see also Conflict
Receptive learning, 41-43, 48
Reeducation (*see* Resocialization)
Reference groups, 130, 131, 134
Referent power, 69, 70, 71, 80, 81,
  155, 156
Reflectivity, 25
Reinforcement, 37, 38, 43-46
Repression, 86
Resistance, to change, 143, 146,
  148, 171

to influence attempts, 56, 57, 119
to leadership, 84
Resocialization of immigrant youth,
98-101, 113-127
Respect, and persuasion, 58
mutual, of teachers and pupils,
160
for teacher, 71
Responsibility, student, 67
teacher, 68
Reward, intrinsic, of problem mastery, 39
power of, 69, 70, 71, 72
in school and student social class,
67, 68
teacher use of, 43, 45, 46, 62
withdrawal of, in resocialization,
116
Rhea, B., 149, 149n, 155, 156, 198
Riots, as stimulus to student protests, 151
Rogers, C., 74, 198
Role, 1-18
behavior, elements of, 98
of leader, 79, 80, 82
changing teacher, 155
conflict, 7, 8-10, 15, 17, 152, 163
demands, attribution of causality
to, 34
deviate, 95
disturbed child, 95, 96
expectations, 84, 85, 148, 152
for deviate, 95, 96
integration, 141, 142
interrelations, 139
learning, 98-138
models, 116, 120, 121, 123, 124,
125, 131, 132
perception, 4, 6
performance, 3, 4, 5, 93, 140
perspective, 1-18
playing techniques, 55, 56
pressures, 35, 136, 142
relationships, 146

requirements, 118
retarded child, 95, 96
student, 11-15, 152, 156
supervisor, 146
taking on new, 101 (see also Resocialization)
teacher, 3-11, 65, 119, 144, 145,
164
theory, 1-18
training, of teachers, 10, 11
Rosen, B. C., 102, 198
Rosencranz, H. A., 190
Rosenthal, R., 12, 12n, 13, 29, 198
Ross, D., 47, 198
Rote learning, 41, 42, 43
Rules, breaking of, 89
inappropriate, 91
internalized, 16
Ryan, J. J., III, 196

St. John, N. H., 108, 194
Sanctions, 7, 48, 49
Sanford, R. N., 189
Schachter, S., 87, 198
School, administrators, 15-17, 148
board, 143
and family socialization, 101-113
inadequacies of, 151, 186, 187
norms, 89
relevance of, 90, 104, 150, 184
structure, changing, 160-165, 171
vulnerability of, 143, 148
Secord, P. F., 17n, 198
Segregated classes for retarded, 95,
96
Seidenberg, B., 192, 195, 196
Self, esteem and persuasibility, 60
evaluation of, student, 96, 106,
107, 108, 109
mortification of, 94
Self-concept, 12, 33, 94
Self-directed learning, 40
Self-fulfilling prophecy, 29, 97, 109
Sensitivity, interpersonal, 164, 165

training, 167, 168
see also Person perception
Shipman, V., 105n, 194
Sieber, S. D., 142n, 144, 144n, 198
"Significant other person," 103
Simulation, in change attempts, 170, 175, 176
in instructional games, 39, 90
Skills, educational, acquiring of, 104-106
Skinner, B. F., 43, 198
Smith, F. F., Jr., 190
Social adjustment problems, 88
Social change, rapid, 100, 113, 114, 139
Social class, bias of schools and teachers, 14
and mother's teaching style, 63
and rebellion in high school, 90
of schools, and teacher influence, 67, 68
of student and teacher credibility, 60, 150
and threat effectiveness, 51
values, perceived, 137
Social conditions and school failure, 34, 35
Social-emotional leadership, 69, 72, 73
Social psychologist, applied, 173
Social support, 53, 55, 91
Socialization, 98-138
agencies, 99-101
agent, teacher as, 106, 107, 134, 135, 136,138
college, 127-138
into deviant role, 95
family and school, 101-113
immigrant, 98-101, 113-127
into teacher role, 11
Special classes for retarded, 95, 96
Speech of Negro students, teacher reaction to, 107, 108
Spicker, H. H., 96, 194

Staff development, 178
Standards, failure to meet, 89 (*see also* Deviance)
Status, of communicator, 61
handicapped child's recognition of low, 94
insecurity of teachers, 144, 146, 148
Stereotypes, 29-33
Stigma, 92, 93, 94
Stinchcombe, A. L., 89, 90, 91, 199
Stone, G. C., 193
Strodbeck, F. L., 63, 199
Structure of school, changing the, 160-165, 171
Student activism, 185
Student isolation from teachers, 152
Student leadership, 80
Student peer groups, 128
Student power, 187
Student-centered teaching, 67, 82-84
Summerhill, 67, 68
Supervision of teachers, 145
Surveillance by teacher, 70
Survey feedback as change technique, 167

Taft, R. A., 115, 199
Taylor, R. M., 8, 194
Teachable groupings, 26
Teacher, competence of, 142
control by, and coercion, 62
in discovery learning, 40
in exposition, 42
and leadership style, 74, 83
and reinforcement, 43, 44
and social class of schools, 154, 155
using threat, 51, 52
expectations of, 107, 109, 123
incompetence of, 108
leadership of, 80, 81
peer groups of, 146
perception of deviance by, 89

as professional, 148
pupil interaction with, 36, 45, 83, 106-120
and role, 3-11
  conflicts, 8-10
  expectations, 95, 96
  others' perception of, 4-7
  vs. persuader role, 8
  in resocialization, 119
  and resistance to innovations, 144, 145
  and restructuring of school, 164
  and satisfaction of students, 65
  tension, 7, 9
  training, 11
self-image of, 146
stereotype of, 32, 33
training of, 35
vulnerability of, 153
Teacher behavior, low
  visibility of, 140-142, 146, 148
Teacher-centered leadership, 82-84
Teaching, direct, 40-42, 48
  machine, 36, 37, 44, 49, 140, 144, 145
  vs. selling, 63
  structured, 74
  style of, 62, 63
Television, 63
Tests *vs.* continual evaluation, 44
Thailand schools, resocialization in, 115-125
Thelen, H. A., 26, 199
Thomas, F. J., 190
Thought patterns, influence of
  teaching style on, 62, 63, 64
Threat, teacher use of, 51-53, 70
Tracking system, 14, 96, 109
Tutoring, and computer assisted instruction, 38
Twyman, P., 6, 7, 199

Underachievement of Negro youth, 104-110

Understanding (*see* Person perception)
Unions, teachers', 153
Urban experiments, 175
Urban schools, 108, 123, 137, 158

Values, core cultural, 57
  on democratic leadership, 81
  educational, acquiring of, 104-106
  internalization of, 92, 120
  and personal and rational choice, 58
  and persuasion, 63
  of school, 50, 67, 68
  social class, and high school rebellion, 90
Verbal interaction, via books, 36
  in programmed instruction, 37
Veroff, J., 104, 199

Wallace, W. L., 132, 133n, 199
Wapner, S., 199
Warwick, D., 132, 198
Watson, G., 197
Watson, J., 196
Weiby, M., 34, 195
Weiss, W., 194
Westley, B., 196
Wheeler, S., 190
White, R. K., 74-82, 196, 199
Willower, D., 154, 199
Win-lose encounters, 159, 163
Winterbottom, M. R., 102, 199
Witkin, H. A., 24, 199
Wittes, S., 149n
Workshop on school problems, 173-185
Wright, B., 93, 99

Youth consultants, 177, 178, 183

Zander, A., 193
Zigler, E., 99n, 199